Lay Leaders in Catholic Higher Education

LAY LEADERS IN CATHOLIC HIGHER EDUCATION

An Emerging Paradigm for the Twenty-First Century

Edited by
Anthony J. Cernera

Sacred Heart University Press
Fairfield, Connecticut

Lay Leaders in Catholic Higher Education
An Emerging Paradigm for the Twenty-First Century

Edited by Anthony J. Cernera

Library of Congress Control Number: 2004116762
ISBN 1-888112-10-7 (hardcover)

Contents

PART III
SPIRITUALITY AND LAY LEADERS IN ACADEME

PART IV
LAY LEADERS: ISSUES AND PERSPECTIVES

Introduction

ANTHONY J. CERNERA

Each year numerous conferences and symposia are sponsored on college and university campuses. One such conference drew over 180 senior-level educators, administrators, university trustees, and leaders of religious communities, including twenty-six Catholic college presidents, to Sacred Heart University, Fairfield, Connecticut, from June 13-15, 2003. Jointly sponsored by the university and the Association of Catholic Colleges and Universities, "Lay Leaders in Catholic Higher Education: An Emerging Paradigm for the Twenty-First Century" included presentations, collaborative working groups, discussions of the theological and spiritual dimensions of effective leadership within Catholic higher education, presentations of models of success in lay leadership, and opportunities for prayer and worship.

In addition to the expected excellent and scholarly dialogue, something dramatic happened. Our intuitions and anecdotal observations about the state of lay leaders in Catholic higher education were confirmed. A study presented at the conference said that for the first time, lay people now outnumber clergy and members of religious orders as presidents of Catholic colleges and universities. The report, "Leadership and the Age of the Laity: Emerging Patterns in Catholic Higher Education," was based on a survey of the country's 222 Catholic college and university presidents, of whom 116 are lay. The authors, Melanie M. Morey and Rev. Dennis H. Holtschneider, presented their findings on the first evening of the conference. Of the many observations made in the report, I would like to concentrate on three points of particular interest as well as strategic concern for the future development of lay leaders that were confirmed by the study and discussed by the participants of the Lay Leaders in Catholic Higher Education conference.

First, the number of lay leaders is growing and is likely to continue to grow. The implications of this new trend have yet to unfold but lay leaders will undoubtedly add a new and added dimension to the conversations and processes by which the Church and religious congregations interact with college presidents. Second, most lay presidents of Catholic colleges and universities have come to their job with little formal theological training (four percent have earned a terminal degree in theological studies). This would seem to present a challenge to being an effective leader of a Catholic institution, especially to one who is charged with promoting the Catholic identity of a university community. Third, most lay presidents resemble their peers at other institutions in terms of their courses of study and career paths, with the most common field of study being education. They also have diverse experiences and perceptions of what it means to be an excellent academic institution. These three points—and many others—were discussed in different ways at the conference and I would like to examine them briefly and discuss some of their implications.

Growing Numbers of Lay Leaders in Catholic Higher Education

Since the Second Vatican Council, lay women and men are assuming greater responsibility for guiding the mission of the Catholic Church in the modern world. This is particularly true in institutions of Catholic higher education in the United States. For example, Sacred Heart University was purposely established by the Most Reverend Walter W. Curtis, then bishop of Bridgeport, in 1963, to be led by lay people. His vision was truly a pioneering one. For the past fifteen years, I have served as the university's president and have lived with the challenges and blessings of being a lay leader. And now in 2004 my case is not the exception, but more the rule.

In recent times, as Catholic colleges and universities have been developing and growing, there has also been a continuing decline in the numbers of religious men and women. The changing sponsorship-governance relationships between religious institutes and congregations and their college and university communities is the direct result of the aging of and decrease in numbers of qualified religious to staff these institutions. This shift in demographics has prompted a number of Catholic religious congregations and colleges to be involved in restructuring processes that intend to charge the laity with significant leadership responsibilities. Some Catholic colleges have become private institutions, and still others, due to the dramatic changes in the size, scope, and costs associated with higher education, have merged with other schools or closed their doors altogether. However, the story is not as bleak as some might suggest, since several new Catholic colleges are also being built.

But what will this mean for lay leaders to promote the relationship of Catholic colleges and universities with the local and universal Church? Surely a respectful seeking of the guidance of the Holy Spirit will assist in the task of integrating the teachings and spirit of Vatican II without being pulled back to a former time of fear and exclusion.

Catholic Identity

As noted above, most lay presidents come to the job with little formal theological training. If one is the leader of a Catholic institution, then one must know or be surrounded by people who are attentive to the Catholic intellectual tradition and be able to articulate a Catholic identity beyond anecdotal stories of youth and the superficial nostalgia of the good old days. But these are also good and promising days. Decisions of core curriculum, faculty hiring, research funding, and the practices, policies, and procedures with which we treat each other are exciting and critical opportunities for us to cultivate and renew our university communities with a Catholic character and heritage.

But should we not be wary of losing our Catholic identity, especially if our leaders have little formal theological training? The document *Ex Corde Ecclesiae* seems to be an effort by the Vatican to stop or even reverse the trend towards religious disengagement in American Catholic institutions. Such efforts are important.

Works by Douglas Sloan, Lawrence Soley, and, most notably, James T. Burtchaell, who studied the development of seventeen American colleges and universities that were founded by prominent churches, all lament the disengagement of a variety of schools from their founding religious vision to become nonsectarian.[1]

Of course, Catholic lay presidents' life experiences will necessarily cause them to articulate the Catholic identity of their communities in different ways from their religious counterparts. In fact, the most interesting part of this unfolding history of lay leaders is that the presidency and the vast majority of the administrators, faculty, and staff of Catholic institutions are now and will continue to come largely from the laity. This requires colleges and universities to do the hard work of clarifying who they are, what they do, and most important, *why* they do these things.

Parts II and III of this volume present strategies to help us begin thinking about and fostering theological and spiritual education for lay leaders. The complexities of Church-university relations are still being debated, as is the proper role and responsibility of lay leaders to provide experiences and resources that promote spiritual growth. These issues will persist and increase in importance as diocesan and parish resources decrease.

In her book, *Negotiating Identity: Catholic Higher Education since 1960*, Alice Gallin, argues that much work remains to be done in articulating the characteristics that distinguish institutions as Catholic.[2] Establishing a powerful connection of vision, mission, and identity is the direct responsibility of sponsors and leaders. They will need to retain that which is historically important to the institution/community as well as adapt to the new opportunities of the future. To neglect either the past or future in the present is to risk an institutional identity crisis that could negatively impact enrollment and alumni/ae support.

Catholic Leadership in Action

Lay presidents have talents that distinguish them, one of which is that they are able to draw good people around them to care for the mission of their institutions. It should prove interesting to observe the ways that lay leaders will engage the American culture and academy. Many have attended non-Catholic universities and presume, for example, that respect for individual rights, tolerance, justice, pluralism, and academic freedom are necessary conditions for truth to be discovered and wisdom to be lived. These leaders will not have the same kinds of wariness towards modernity and apprehensiveness that such conditions, if unleashed to the extreme, could obscure or destroy the very nature of education. Jaroslav Pelikan has rightly lamented that many universities bracket or ignore the religious areas of study and thereby offer students an inadequate and shallow form of knowledge and education.[3]

There should be no doubt at any of our institutions that we are unabashedly Catholic, that these are places where Jesus and the Church are found. Whether in the classroom, on the fields, in the residence halls, or serving the poor in the community, the language and life of faith is understood as necessarily integrated into all that we do and all we are.

As new models of Catholic higher education leadership emerge, it will continue to be very difficult for religious congregations to move from "doing" the majority of the apostolic work to "guiding," as others pick up the torch in planning and practice. Vatican II's *Perfectae Caritas*, as well as Pope Paul VI's *Ecclesiae Sanctae* and *Evangelica Testificatio*, identify religious life as a response to a call by God to meet the needs of the Church. The Holy Spirit is still very much alive and calling religious congregations to serve in many ways. The training and recruitment of religious congregational members for the ministry in colleges and universities is important, but will not adequately address the coming challenge. The efforts of religious and laity working together must be more than creating figure head appointments with veto power.

Some universities are beginning to take a serious look at ways to better prepare lay presidents and administrators to lead Catholic institutions. Boston College started an institute in 2001 to help administrators of Catholic colleges deal with the transition from religious to lay leadership. Catholic colleges and universities will need to develop programs for students, employees, faculty, parents, and trustees that promote theological education, spiritual development, ethical reflection, leadership development, and mission effectiveness.

The torch of Catholic higher education is not a static possession to be fearfully guarded, but a vision and way of life, fueled by the past, confidently carried by those who dare, like those before us, to bring Christ's faith, hope, and love into the future. I know we all look forward to the continued efforts to improve Catholic higher education. The recent conference at Sacred Heart University provides us with a new and hope-filled point of departure, and this present volume is a further step along the way. I hope that what you read here, which attempts to capture and expand on the conference presentations and conversations, will spur all of us to continue to engage our students and our Church as we explore and live out the emerging paradigm of lay leadership.

A special word of thanks is due to David L. Coppola, executive assistant to the president of Sacred Heart University, Sidney Gottlieb, professor of Media Studies and Digital Culture at Sacred Heart University, and Christopher J. Sheehan, Sacred Heart University writer and editor, for their efforts in bringing this work to completion.

Notes

1. Douglas Sloan, *Faith and Knowledge: Mainline Protestantism and American Higher Education* (London: Westminster/John Knox Press, 1994); Lawrence Soley, *Leasing the Ivory Tower: The Corporate Takeover of Academia* (Westport, CT: Greenwood Press, 1995); James T. Burtchaell, *The Dying of the Light: The Disengagement of Colleges and Universities from Their Christian Churches* (Grand Rapids: Eerdmans, 1998).

2. Alice Gallin, *Negotiating Identity: Catholic Higher Education since 1960* (Notre Dame: University of Notre Dame Press, 2000).

3. Jaroslav Pelikan, *The Idea of a University: A Reexamination* (New Haven: Yale University Press, 1992).

PART I

Describing the Emerging Paradigm: Issues, Challenges, Opportunities

Leadership and the Age of the Laity: Emerging Patterns in Catholic Higher Education

MELANIE M. MOREY AND DENNIS H. HOLTSCHNEIDER

For most of the history of Catholic higher education in the United States, the selection and preparation of leaders was a relatively stable process controlled almost entirely by the bishops and religious congregations that founded and ran the colleges and universities. Over the last thirty-five years lay men and women increasingly entered the leadership pool. As they did, the once well-established pipeline and preparation process for leadership became less well-defined, less certain. Today, more than half the presidents of Catholic colleges and universities are lay persons.[1] The trend toward selecting Catholic lay persons as presidents will continue. We are at a point now where we can compare the backgrounds, aspirations, and career paths of religious and lay presidents—the general focus of this study, which is a key part of its authors' effort to focus on the challenges and promise inherent in the emerging patterns of leadership in American Catholic higher education.[2]

Notes on Methodology

The Leadership Trends Study began in summer 2002 and continued into the fall. Presidents of the country's 222 Catholic colleges and universities were sent twelve-page survey instruments that asked both informational and open-ended questions about presidential backgrounds and aspirations. The surveys focused on the institutional challenges presidents are facing and will face in the near future, as well as on how they understand Catholic higher education as an enterprise and how it is likely to develop over the next ten years. Fifty-five percent of the surveys were completed and returned.

In order to position this study in relation to the broader landscape of American higher education, we asked a series of questions that mirrored questions posed in the American Council on Education's recently published survey.[3] The ACE data were then used to compare the presidents of Catholic colleges and universities with their peers in all areas of American higher education.[4]

Findings

Two types of results emerge from this study. One is almost purely factual and statistical while the second is more interpretive. Since the survey covers over 55% of all presidents and because in this paper we focus on major differences between religious and lay presidents, the factual, statistical results speak largely for themselves. For the interpretive results, we will present arguments and analysis to justify our interpretation.

The seven principal factual findings presented in this paper represent a provocative portrait of leadership in Catholic higher education. Interestingly, the portrait that emerges contravenes much of the conventional wisdom that swirls in the atmosphere and peppers conversations of those attentive to this sector of American higher education.

It might be possible, when listening to public discourse on the topic, to believe that there is something unique about Catholic college and university presidents, compared to their counterparts in other colleges and universities, and that women are coming into their own in leadership in all institutional arenas in higher learning. It also might be possible to believe that faculty, who play a central role in colleges and universities and are the primary and most long-term collegiate educators, are committed to enriching the Catholic character, identity, and mission of the institutions they serve. Public discourse sometimes suggests that lay persons are being chosen over religious men and women to lead Catholic colleges and universities and that they are adequately prepared in terms of religious background and training for their presidential tasks. The conversation could suggest that presidents have emerged from ten years of painful and conflicted interaction around all aspects of *Ex Corde Ecclesiae* with little desire for a relationship with their local ordinaries. And, finally, with all the focus on and discussion of Catholic identity and mission, it would seem natural that some common definitions and clarity of purpose had been achieved. The findings of this study challenge all these perceptions.

Along with the factual findings, two interpretive conclusions emerge from this study. First, the boards of trustees who hire presidents have not yet identified minimum standards of religious education and training they deem essential for all Catholic college and university presidents. Second, the increasing dominance of lay persons in the leadership of Catholic colleges and universities has had an ambiguous impact, at best, in terms of the ideological divides in Catholic higher education. Conservative, liberal, and middle of the road lay men and women are assuming leadership positions in institutions that represent the full range of the ideological spectrum. The involvement of lay persons has resulted in neither a general trend toward any one type of leader nor a tilt toward a particular institutional ideology.

Who are the Catholic college and university presidents?

> *Finding 1: As a cohort, Catholic college and university presidents increasingly resemble their presidential peers elsewhere in U.S. higher education.*

Catholic college presidents were generally religious and/or priests in past years, and because of this they differed as a cohort from their presidential peers at other institutions in notable ways. These differences often could be seen in the types of degrees they held, their fields of study and expertise, their career paths, reasons they sought or accepted a presidency, and, perhaps most notably, in their gender mix. As Catholic institutions of higher education have become increasingly led by lay people, these differences are fading.

Fields of Study

Perhaps the most obvious example of the trend is in the area of a president's field of study. Thirty-four percent of the religious presidents, for example, have theology/religious studies degrees, while only 4% of lay presidents have concentrated in theological studies. That is actually less than their peers in the ACE study of presidents, where 7% of presidents have terminal degrees in religion or theology.[5]

After theology, the second-most common major field of study for presidents who are religious is education, where 30% of religious presidents have education degrees. Forty-three percent of lay Catholic college presidents have graduate education degrees, making that the most common field of study for lay presidents. Forty-three percent mirrors exactly the national proportion of presidents with education degrees in American higher education.[6] Lay presidents and religious presidents have chosen fields in the humanities in similar numbers (20% lay; 18% religious), but lay people are far more likely to have concentrated in the professions (20% lay; 7% religious).

The fact that only 4% of lay presidents have concentrated in theological studies, compared to 34% of their religious counterparts, suggests that the future leadership of Catholic colleges and universities will be far less likely to have formal theological training at an advanced level than previous generations of presidents who, as members of religious congregations were more apt to be so schooled.

It is not surprising that all presidents who are religious report having formal religious training and formation. What is surprising, however, is that 27% of lay presidents had some previous formal religious formation while training to become priests or religious. This level of religious formation among lay leaders has contributed to religious coherence during the transition from religious to lay leadership. Because the stream of lay leaders who once spent time in religious formation has slowed to a trickle, this source of religious coherence will disappear.

Career Paths

Differences also can be noticed in the career tracks lay and religious take toward their first presidencies. Sixty-two percent of religious presidents report having held an administrative post before assuming a presidency, while 81% of lay presidents first participated in a search while serving in an administrative post. This again matches the exact proportion reported in the 2001 ACE study of presidents, where 82% of presidents held administrative posts before assuming a presidency.[7] It also is more likely that lay people served as academic officers prior to their first presidential search, but not by a large margin: 43% of lay presidents came from academic administration, while 37% of religious served as academic officers before coming to a presidency. Religious presidents were more likely to come to a search directly from a faculty position (15% religious; 9% lay). Religious presidents also were more likely to come from outside higher education altogether (22% religious; 5% lay).

When asked why they first considered seeking a presidency at this time in their lives, 24% of religious presidents responded using religious language such as "advancing the mission," "obedience to the request of a superior," and "service to the church." Four percent of lay presidents used such language in their responses. On the other hand, 67% of lay presidents listed professional and practical considerations in weighing a possible presidential bid, such as the "time was right," "the location of the institution was agreeable," or they "were interested in and/or prepared to meet the challenges of the presidency," whereas only 30% of religious presidents reported considering such factors prior to accepting a presidency.

These differences persist when presidents are asked why they ultimately chose to accept the offer of a presidency. Slightly over a third of the responses of religious presidents (35%) spoke of such things as the Catholic identity of the institution, the opportunity to contribute to the church, religious commitment, values, mission, service, the will of God, and/or responsibility and commitment to the founding congregation. Similar motivations represented only 19% of the responses of lay presidents. For 54% of all lay presidents, professional and practical considerations such as "being prepared or ready," "a great opportunity," "location," "good fit," or "the time was right" were the most commonly mentioned reasons for accepting a presidency. For religious presidents, 36% spoke of such matters.[8]

The fact that lay presidents were far less likely to explain their reasons for accepting a presidency in terms of religious mission, sense of vocation, or categories of service should not necessarily be interpreted to mean they do not have religious motivation. Nevertheless, it is striking that even when answering a survey that clearly focused on the religious mission of their institutions, lay presidents were far less likely to speak in such terms.

Lay presidents are less likely than their religious counterparts to have theology degrees; they are less likely to have doctoral degrees in the arts or sciences, and they are less likely to have served in other positions at the institution at which they are currently president. Lay presidents are less likely to have come to the presidency directly from a faculty position or from a position outside higher education altogether and more likely to have education or professional degrees. Lay presidents are more likely to have held an administrative post prior to being appointed president, and are more likely to explain their reasons for accepting a presidency in terms of professional and practical considerations. In all these matters, lay presidents of Catholic colleges and universities more closely resemble their presidential peers at non-Catholic institutions than do their religious counterparts in Catholic higher education.

Finding 2: Women are disappearing from the presidency in Catholic colleges and universities.

Across the landscape of American higher education, men are more likely than women to be presidents. In Catholic colleges and universities, males dominate in numbers, but to a lesser extent. The ACE study reports that 79% of college and university presidents are men, while 21% are women. By contrast, the LTS reports that only 64% of presidents are men, while 36% are women. On the face of it, the Catholic sector appears a somewhat more hospitable environment than higher education in general for women to exercise presidential leadership. Appearances are deceiving, however, if one fails to appreciate the historical preeminence of women presidents in Catholic institutions founded by women's religious congregations.

In 1967, 169 of the 266 Catholic colleges and universities open to lay enrollment (64%) were founded by women religious, and all of these were led by female members of the founding religious congregations.[9] In 2002-03, according to LTS findings, about a third of Catholic colleges and universities had women presidents. So, while the percentage of women presidents is far greater in Catholic higher education than in higher education nationally, the trend lines for each group are headed in decidedly different directions. The ACE study reports that in the years 1986-2001 the percentage of women presidents more than doubled. In the last thirty-five years the percentage of women presidents in Catholic higher education, on the other hand, has been steadily decreasing.

In American higher education, generally, the number of women presidents is on the rise in doctorate-granting institutions.[10] That is not the case in Catholic higher education. According to the ACE study, in 1986 only 4.3% of public doctorate-granting institutions had women presidents. In that same year 2.9% of the private doctorate-granting institutions were led by women. By 2001 significant gains were made by women nationally. Among public doctorate-granting institutions, 15.7% had women presidents, and 8.9% of similar private institutions also were led by women.[11] By contrast, in 2003 only one of the Catholic doctorate-granting universities is led by a woman president.[12]

In the past two years, thirty new presidents have been named at Catholic colleges and universities in the United States.[13] Twenty-one of the presidents named, 70%, were men and nine were women. Women presidents were appointed only in those institutions founded by women religious, and, among those institutions, fully 52%, or ten institutions, appointed men to lead them.[14]

Clearly women are making inroads in the leadership ranks in American higher education. At Catholic institutions, however, their historic place is eroding. At this point it is difficult to know if, when, or where the trend line for Catholic institutions will bottom out and the one for higher education nationally will peak. Both trends could settle within a reasonable striking distance of each other or continue until a wide gap emerges. For the moment, however, we can report only the trend—one that looks less promising for women in Catholic higher education than in American higher education more generally.

Finding 3: Lay persons infrequently emerge as presidents from finalist pools containing members of the founding religious congregation.

Searches producing lay presidents, by and large, have no founding congregation members in the finalist pool.[15] When asked if there were any founding congregation members in the finalist pool from which they were chosen president, 90% of lay presidents said there were not. If the candidate pool consisted of all lay professionals, then obviously a lay person was chosen. That was the case for 90% of the lay presidents in this study. Only 4% of all the presidents responding to LTS, however, were lay presidents chosen over congregational finalists. There is an apparent preference among boards for presidents who are members of founding religious congregations. Generally speaking, this apparent preference persists even when these religious men and women have less administrative experience than lay finalists.

In response to questions about career path, 81% of lay presidents indicated serving in an administrative post when first considered for a presidency, whereas only 62% of religious presidents had been similarly employed. Religious presidents, on the other hand, were more likely to come to a search directly from a faculty position (15% religious; 9% lay). Religious presidents were also far more likely than lay presidents to come to a presidency from outside higher education (22% religious; 5% lay).

It is at least curious that at a time in the nation when seasoned higher education administrators are increasingly in demand to fill presidential posts, selection committees at Catholic colleges and universities are willing to go directly into the faculty or outside higher education altogether to find a religious president.[16] Any number of reasons might explain this counter-intuitive preference, but commitment to loyalty, legitimacy, literacy, and formal religious formation seem particularly plausible.

Loyalty to the founding congregation is one obvious reason some boards might prefer religious to lay people for a presidency. Having a member of the founding congregation as president is an obvious and direct way to support and enhance the founding heritage and legacy of the institution. This kind of loyalty emerges even in situations in which a board chooses a lay person. When boards do hire lay men or women, they often hire those who once had some sustained and real contact with the congregational charism, individuals (for example, who have studied or worked at one of the founding congregation's institutions).

While congregational loyalty may be the motivation in some circumstances, it cannot fully explain the apparent preference for religious presidents. There are a number of circumstances in which the religious president chosen is not a member of the founding congregation and has little or no connection with that congregation or the college itself. In those cases religious status, not congregational affiliation, seems to be the more significant factor.

A presumption of legitimacy might also underlie the selection of religious for leadership at Catholic colleges and universities. Religious men and women by their very presence have provided a vital component of Catholic institutional identity in all of their institutional ministries. Patricia Wittberg points out that

> Catholic hospitals, schools, and social-work agencies derived their religious identity primarily from the presence of religious congregations. Religious nurses, teachers, and social workers, all fully habited, served as living icons of the spiritual character of these institutions. . . . Without pointing to the congregation's presence, it would have been hard for a school or hospital to articulate what made it Catholic. Until the mid 1960s, however, the two were so intertwined that the question never even arose.[17]

At a time when Catholic identity is at best an illusive concept, this iconic presence remains a powerful legitimating factor that simply is not available to lay persons in the Church.

Religious literacy is another factor that might enhance the candidacy of religious men and women in a presidential search. Selection committees recognize that men and women religious have strong academic backgrounds in theology and philosophy, something quite rare among most lay persons. In situations in which leadership for Catholic character and mission are primary considerations, religious candidates could well have a significant edge over their lay colleagues because of this training.

The fact that formal religious formation may play an even more important role than theological literacy in a board's presidential hiring decisions is born out in the study. Data indicate that when boards hire lay presidents, they appear to give preference to former religious or individuals who once studied in a religious formation program. They do not, however, give preference to laity with religious studies or theology degrees. It is spiritual formation and congregational connection, not theological literacy, which attracts boards to men and women religious and ex-religious. These kinds of commitments and connections can be assumed with religious, but must be demonstrated by lay candidates.

> *Finding 4: There is a significant lack of formal theological and spiritual preparation among presidents. There is also widespread agreement among presidents that inadequate lay preparation presents a problem for the future of Catholic higher education. Despite this, few lay presidents (9%) report that they personally feel ill-equipped to lead the religious mission of their institutions.*

Perceptions

Forty percent of presidents indicated that there is something lacking in the effective preparation, development, and empowerment of lay leadership in Catholic higher education. Presidents, both lay and religious, fear that without serious attention to this dimension the Catholic and congregational identity and mission of these institutions will fade away. One religious president believes, "As priests, brothers, and nuns age and decline in numbers, the need for informed, competent administrators in Catholic higher education will become more acute. Compounding this problem is the limited pool of potential lay leaders who are familiar with the Catholic religious and educational heritage." This particular position is most often articulated by religious presidents who truly wonder whether lay leadership is up to the task of leadership for Catholic character, mission, and identity given their present levels of education and preparation.

When asked to describe the areas of leadership they perceived themselves most prepared to assume the first day they began their presidency and the areas of leadership they felt least prepared to assume, small differences emerged between lay and religious presidents. Their responses fell into three general categories: organizational leadership—the preparation necessary to run any complex organization, educational or otherwise; faculty and academic culture—elements specific to higher education; and religious character, mission, and identity—elements unique to Catholic colleges and universities.

When speaking of the ways in which they felt best prepared, most presidents chose to list items related to the day-to-day operations of their institutions, such as budgeting and financial management, advancement, public relations, admissions, technology, strategic planning, staff development, personnel management, and overall leadership (68% lay, 58% religious). A lesser number reported that they felt very well-prepared to negotiate the faculty and academic culture of their institutions (20% lay, 30% religious). A few mentioned feeling well-prepared to lead the religious mission of their colleges (9% lay, 11% religious).

The same rank order repeated itself when presidents reported the areas of leadership they felt least prepared to assume. They spoke most frequently of feeling ill-equipped to solve organizational difficulties related to financial crises, enrollment management, and most particularly, institutional fund-raising. This was exacerbated by the lack of privacy and pervasive loneliness of a job many came to understand only after assuming their roles (67% lay, 76% religious). Particular examples of academic culture and faculty resistance were cited far less often than organizational issues by religious presidents (16%) and lay presidents (19%) as areas for which they felt ill-prepared.

In the area of religious character, mission, and identity, only 7% of religious presidents and 9% of lay presidents reported feeling ill-prepared. (There were four "amazing" presidents, one religious and three lay, who felt ill-prepared for nothing, and one lone lay president who claimed that in the first year of the presidency everything was overwhelming.)

Preparation

Lay and religious presidents responding to the LTS reported very different preparation for leading the religious mission of their institutions. All religious presidents reported having taken undergraduate theology and philosophy courses, and 61% of them have graduate degrees in theological or religious studies. All of the religious presidents also have participated in formal religious formation within their congregations or in the seminary. Sixty-three percent of this group claimed further participation in ongoing formation programs such as institutes or special courses.

Sixteen percent of lay presidents have graduate level degrees in theological or religious studies. Twenty-seven percent have had some formal religious formation within seminaries or religious congregations, and 45% of lay presidents, slightly less than half, have taken at least one undergraduate theology and philosophy course. That means, however, that 55% of lay presidents have no religious training beyond high school, while 30% of lay presidents report no religious or theological education of any kind.

The differences between these two groups are striking. For the most part, however, lay presidents do not see their lack of religious knowledge and formation as a particular weakness in terms of their own presidency. It is unclear why this is the case. Perhaps critical financial, enrollment, or advancement issues loom so large that the Catholic character and mission of the institution pales in comparison. Some presidents may have compensated for their own limitations in this area by delegating the responsibility to others in the institution. Other presidents may find responsibilities in this area so unspecific and vague that their own limitations pose no real challenge to a sense of professional adequacy.

At the same time, some presidents who dismiss a lack of preparation as a negative influence in their own presidency clearly identify it as a problem for Catholic higher education as a whole.

There are different ways of looking at this seeming contradiction. Some presidents are, in fact, well-prepared themselves and the general trend has no particular application in their case. It is also quite possible that presidents were unwilling to draw the obvious personal conclusion about their own preparation gaps in a national survey. Finally, it is possible that, like most of us, Catholic college and university presidents have an uncanny ability to see the splinter in another's eye while missing the plank in their own. Whatever the reasons for the personal optimism, the data clearly indicate that lay presidents lack significant preparation for leadership in the areas of mission and identity, and, at least in general terms, identify this gap as a serious problem for the future of Catholic higher education, but not for themselves individually.

Addressing the Preparation Gap

While there might be reasons for an institution to hire a president with little preparation for identity and mission leadership, it hardly seems reasonable to leave this leadership gap unattended. Unfortunately, there is little concerted effort made by institutions to educate presidents in any systematic way.

When asked how they became educated about the mission and heritage of the institution they lead, only 15% of the respondents indicated participation in any formal congregation- or institution-sponsored program. None indicated participation in any formal external program. Fifty-six percent of the responses of religious presidents indicated previous experience or education including religious formation as the way they were educated about heritage and mission. Only 10% of lay presidents' responses fell into this category. Seventy-seven percent of lay presidents claimed they were self-taught in the areas of heritage and mission, and 83.5% of all their responses indicated informal interaction or personal reading as the source of their knowledge about the religious history, character, and mission of the college or university at which they serve as chief executive officer.

There are very few formal programs established within congregations or at colleges and universities to bring a president up to speed. Likewise, there is a paucity of programs outside individual institutions that offer formal preparation for mission and identity leadership. With so few opportunities or programs in existence, presidents are largely left to their own devices when it comes to preparing to lead their institutions in the one truly unique aspect of their heritage and mission.

Lay and religious presidents have distinctly different levels of preparation for leadership in the area of Catholic heritage, tradition, and identity. With little or no formal preparation, formation, or study, lay men and women enter Catholic college and university presidencies with a distinct leadership disadvantage. It would seem that this lack of religious education and formation could have a negative impact on the enterprise of Catholic higher education. Presidents, however, do not seem convinced, nor do the institutions they serve.

Contending with Mission

Finding 5: Forty-one percent of religious and 26% of lay presidents find the phrases "Catholic identity" and "Catholic intellectual tradition" to be fuzzy concepts that lack sufficient vitality on campuses. They want clearer definitions so they can develop strategies to effectively enhance this unique identity on their own campuses.

Presidents asked, "How do we understand mission as more than rhetoric and historical tradition? How do we avoid the mission becoming so diffuse or diluted [that] the institution becomes disconnected from its purpose?" With a desire "to stop blowing in the wind and stand for something," many presidents agree that Catholic colleges and universities must "maintain a Catholic identity, being precise about what that identity means and the reasons for the importance of sustaining Catholic higher education." They believe that without clear definition and strategic attention, there is no hope a Catholic intellectual tradition will thrive as the heart of their institutions.

Finding 6: Presidents desire a more supportive working relationship with the hierarchical church but find such a relationship elusive and complex. Female presidents (27%) identify this more often than male presidents (13%). Lay presidents (27%) identify this more often than their religious counterparts (10%).

The *Ex Corde Ecclesiae* discussion over the last ten years compounded the tension between the Church and presidents. Some presidents believe that it remains a potential arena of mischief that will only further frustrate their relationship with the Church. Other presidents see this process, albeit painful and prickly, as having forced a conversation that otherwise would have been avoided.

When asked to list the most important challenges facing Catholic higher education, 18% of presidents stated that a workable relationship with the organizational Church, one that is a support to the enterprise rather than an impediment, is important for assuring the vibrancy of Catholic higher education in the United States. They want to move on and away from the bitterness and lack of trust that often characterized their relationships with the organizational Church over the past decade and identify strategies for creating deeper appreciation and support between both parties. At the same time, they seek respect for the contributions their institutions make to the Church. These presidents believe that a continuation of a brittle standoff between colleges and hierarchical authorities will serve no one's purposes.

The more frequent concern for this on the part of female and lay presidents is important to note. Educated women in this Church have long felt the ironies of working within a system that rarely invites women into the circles of Church decision making. Lay presidents feel only too keenly that the relationship they have to hierarchical leadership is more formalized and distant than the one enjoyed by their religious predecessors. Both groups feel less able than religious to shape the Church's involvement with their institutions.

Finding 7: Presidents all acknowledge the central role faculty play in their institutions. Nevertheless, many presidents, both lay and religious, report that the faculty is an obstacle to effective leadership in the area of Catholic character, mission, and identity.

Presidents in the study were asked about what interferes with their ability to lead the Catholic character and mission of their institutions. The presidents also were asked what they find most difficult about leadership in Catholic higher education. Combining their responses to these two questions proved interesting and revealed that faculty are seen to represent a major obstacle in the area of Catholic character, mission, and identity.

The area of greatest presidential concern in terms of leadership for Catholic identity and mission is the impact of unsupportive faculty and staff on the religious mission of the colleges and universities. Thirty-two percent of lay presidents and 40% of religious presidents report contending with faculty and staff who are tradition-illiterate, hostile toward, or simply uninterested in the Catholic mission and identity of the institutions in which they serve. At one institution the president rather gently points out that interference in his institution comes from "the attitude of some faculty who would like to see the college be an excellent liberal arts institution, but one that is purely secular. Academic excellence alone should be, according to them, the coin of the realm without any reference to or influence by a religious perspective."

Presidents try to deal with the lack of faculty support in a number of ways, in most cases avoiding tackling the issue head-on. One president "continues a background action to try to preserve identity and mission against a growing indifference with smaller and smaller groups of committed professionals." Another placates "some of the old guard faculty, who came in the late 1960s and early 1970s as Catholics, [and] are now bitter toward the Church and resist the label 'Catholic University.' I have found it much more acceptable to them if I emphasize the congregational character of the university."

Interpretive Results

Two interpretive results also emerged from the study. Each is supported by the data, but the assertions are also based on an analysis of the way in which modern Catholic colleges and universities function.

Interpretive Result 1: Boards of trustees have not yet identified minimum standards for religious education and training that lay presidents are expected to meet.

At the same time that lay Catholics started to be selected as presidents of Catholic colleges and universities, a structural change took place in the governance of Catholic institutions of higher education. Prior to the late 1960s, practically all boards of trustees of Catholic institutions were comprised almost exclusively of members of the founding religious congregations. Under the leadership of institutions such as the University of Notre Dame, the College of New Rochelle, and Saint Louis University, lay people were made trustees and assumed leadership roles in governing their institutions.

For the first two or three decades that lay persons assumed such leadership positions, the results were deemed favorable by many. It is well to note that these halcyon years were dominated by deference, particularly in the area of religious identity and mission, to the religious trustees, who represented the interests and concerns of the founding congregations. Reliance on religious trustees has become more problematic over time. Religious congregations have aged and become smaller and are less and less able to appoint member trustees with real knowledge of, or interest in, higher education ministry. Lay trustees have had to become more knowledgeable and tactical about selecting lay presidents. While they have become more proficient in terms of assessing the capacity and fit of candidates in traditional areas of executive leadership, their expectations regarding mission and identity leadership have remained vague, unfocused, and largely unarticulated.

If the people who hire them remain unable to define appropriate religious qualifications for Catholic college presidents, it is unlikely there will be any consensus about what background should be deemed adequate for these leadership roles. If this lack of clarity among trustees continues, the chances for mission drift only compound.

Interpretive Result 2: Ideological divisions are well-known in American Catholic higher education today. There is no

> *indication that the increasing dominance of lay persons in the leadership of Catholic institutions of higher education will do anything to diminish these stark differences. In fact, they may actually intensify.*

The Catholic ideological wars that presidents endure are a fact of life that presidents will, most likely, have to live with for the foreseeable future. The frustration that presidents express in response to these pitched battles ranges from slightly irritated, to beleaguered, to downright indignant. Interestingly, the frustration seems to have gender overtones and is far more of a burden to men than women. Only 9% of women presidents claim they are plagued by the orthodoxy wars, while 24% of male presidents say they find the attacks from the left and the right to be major obstacles to leadership.

One of the milder presidential assessments of ideological difficulties maintains that the most taxing aspect of Catholic institutional leadership is "being in the middle between ultra-conservative Catholics who really don't understand the university's role and those who may understand it but are opposed." A more outraged president rails against the

> chronic and often scandalous pressure and interference from the right wing, the self-appointed third-party groups that the bishops should shut down in the name of the Church. Allowing faculty and administrators to be subjected to and harassed by the intemperate, intolerant, and ignorant rants of the righteous is both disappointing and discouraging when we work so hard to keep our institutions going. Instead of having our contributions recognized and praised, we are often viewed with suspicion and treated as "fair game" by the self-appointed watchdogs who would hardly survive a day in our trenches.

What is of particular interest about the internal and external "Catholicity police" is the fact that, by and large, they are lay people. From outspoken faculty on the one side who deride the incursion of church in the academy to the members of the Cardinal Newman Society on the other who constantly call fidelity fouls, the loudest proponents of Catholic "gotcha!" are lay people who do not wait for religious and clerical permission to level their attacks on the purported misdeeds of Catholic colleges and the presidents who lead them.

Caught between a faculty that is telling them they are too Catholic and conservative Catholics who tell them they are not Catholic enough, presidents feel beaten up by critics who are often less interested in finding solutions than in chastising presidents for failure to meet a preexisting standard. In the face of internal critics championing the academy and external critics challenging their lack of fidelity, every decision becomes a moment for Solomon. Clearly, leadership in the area of Catholic character and mission is not for the faint of heart.

Conclusion

In the survey's final question, presidents were asked to predict the future by indicating the major changes they anticipate for Catholic higher education in five to ten years. For the most part, their responses revealed conventional wisdom. They told us that priests and religious will continue to disappear from Catholic higher education, and that laity will almost entirely eclipse religious leadership and control (33%). They predicted a greater emphasis on the Catholic intellectual tradition and institutional identity (57%). Fifty-four percent of respondents, however, also predicted that there would be fewer Catholic institutions of higher learning in five to ten years, as a result of a series of closures, consolidations, or takeovers of the smaller, more financially fragile institutions. We suspect that the truth of that prediction is more complex than first meets the eye.

Certainly, some colleges will close. Notre Dame College in New Hampshire and Trinity College in Vermont both closed their doors in recent years; Barat College was assumed by DePaul University, and St. Mary's College in Michigan will be acquired by Madonna University in July. Yet, several new Catholic colleges have either recently opened or announced plans to break ground.

Our Lady of Corpus Christi, Ave Maria College and Law School, the two Campion Colleges (in Washington, D.C., and San Francisco), the Catholic Distance University, the College of the South, and most recently De La Salle University, to be located near Sacramento, and the University of Sacramento are additions to the ranks of Catholic colleges and universities. Not all "start-ups" survive, of course, but these new colleges have more than balanced the numbers of Catholic colleges that have recently closed.

Widespread predictions made in the 1970s and 1980s about the terrible fate awaiting much of American higher education were wrong.[18] Grim forecasts about the future for small liberal arts colleges throughout their history also have proven untrustworthy.[19] A careful examination of the history of small colleges shows that many of these institutions have proven to be agile and creative in times of financial crises and, while not becoming wealthy, have managed to stay viable. These are small institutions, and quick, significant change is far easier for them than for larger institutions. Counting them out too quickly could prove unwise.

There is another factor, however, that may prove more tenacious in thinning the ranks of Catholic institutions. Some may choose to abandon their Catholic identity and chart the future as private, non-sectarian institutions. Six—Medaille College, Villa Julie College, Daeman College, Marymount Manhattan College, Nazareth College, and most recently, Marist College—already have chosen to take this path.

A careful reading of survey responses predicting the closure of Catholic colleges cannot help but notice a tone of glib detachment in some of the responses. Some respondents simply write off the smaller colleges, presuming their closure to be of little consequence. This indifference to their fate underestimates the effect their demise could have on the enterprise of Catholic higher education, especially when an institution represents the only Catholic higher education presence in a given region.

A new generation of leadership has arrived in American Catholic higher education in a church that traditionally has identified future leaders from its religious ranks; prepared successive generations of leaders through seminaries, formation programs, and guided career moves; granted moral credibility and leadership through the structures of vows or ordination; and conducted the informal conversations of leadership between bishop and college president in the comfort and context of shared religious profession.

This new generation of presidents, lay professionals, arrives with the extensive preparation, professional experience, and credentials of their lay peers in non-Catholic higher education. With the exception of the transition group of lay men and women who were in formation programs earlier in their careers, the religious background of lay presidents largely ended at confirmation or in required religious studies courses while in college. Reassuringly, lay presidents are committed to enhancing the Catholic nature of their institutions, but nearly all report a lack of clarity on how to proceed. Most report that they have little idea how to understand, assess, manage, or even how to promote Catholic character and identity. In addition, they feel a lack of support within, a sense of attack from without, and a belief that close working relationships with their bishops could be much improved.

These lay professionals assume their presidencies in a historical moment that follows three great transitions in Catholic higher education. As Catholics increasingly migrated into the mainstream, Catholic students began to apply to and attend secular private institutions for the first time in significant numbers in the mid- and late-1960s. The broad stream of Catholic students available to Catholic institutions greatly narrowed. Many single-sex institutions became coeducational. Catholic institutions responded by adjusting their marketing and curricula, and appealing to a broader range of students, many of whom were not Catholic.

Second, as the pressure to compete within mainstream American higher education grew, and as the numbers of trained and available religious diminished, the religious faculty and administration were supplemented and replaced with lay Catholics, as well as non-Catholic professionals. Chosen for their diversity and academic competitiveness, many of these faculty members complemented established, long-term religious faculty and staff.

Once the religious began disappearing from campuses, however, the impact of this more diverse lay faculty with little or no commitment to the religious character of the institution posed a hitherto unanticipated threat to the religious authenticity of Catholic colleges and universities.

The third dramatic transition occurred when Catholic colleges and universities steadily shifted from predominantly religious to lay governance. This happened within the context of a church that to this day provides only basic religious education to laity and considerable formation to religious men and women. Initially, men and women religious continued to set the tone and direction of university policy. As the number of lay trustees increased and their experience broadened, they assumed greater responsibility for the direction of policy.

For at least two decades, trustees have been aware that the leadership of Catholic institutions is passing to lay persons. During most of this period, however, the lay trustees rarely had to think about the religious preparation of presidential candidates who were priests or members of religious congregations. That has changed over time, and lay trustees now have to confront the challenge of assessing adequate religious formation, knowledge, and commitment among potential lay presidents. They are called to do this in challenging times and with no established guidelines to direct them.

This study shows that lay people are increasingly running Catholic institutions of higher education in the United States. Their responses indicate that they care deeply about maintaining the Catholic identity of the institutions. Their views about that Catholic identity, however, cover a broad spectrum of attitudes and assumptions, and they vary greatly in the ways in which they promote the Catholic faith in their own institutions. There is no unanimity and little convergence around practical means to promote the Catholic culture of these institutions.

Many lay presidents genuinely struggle with their own lack of clarity about the Catholic intellectual tradition and about the degree to which they can assert moral and religious leadership over other lay professionals at their institutions. They are unsure about how much explicit focus on religion the market will bear, now that the true market for Catholic higher education is broader than just Catholics. They are also unclear about the particular ways Catholicism might be instilled when Catholicism itself is divided ideologically.

Lay leadership is increasingly the norm, not the exception, in Catholic colleges and universities in the United States. Lay leaders are accepting their increasing responsibility at a time when the structural supports of the past have eroded and the future contours of the enterprise appear dimly in the mist. What is clear is that the shape of Catholic higher education in the future will be in the hands of faith-filled and hardworking lay men and women. Providing a clearer portrait of the emerging patterns of leadership in American Catholic higher education is a place to begin to understand and prepare for that future.

Notes

1. Of the 222 Catholic institutions of higher education in the U.S., 116 have lay presidents and 106 have presidents who are priests or members of religious congregations.

2. In this paper we use the words "religious" and "lay" as they are used in ordinary parlance, though this use does not conform to the meaning of these words as they are used technically within the Roman Catholic Church. According to canon law, a lay person is anyone who is not a bishop, priest, deacon, or someone who has been selected for, but not yet appointed, to one of these positions. Thus, any woman—whether or not she is a nun—is a lay person. In ordinary parlance, a nun is not considered a lay person because she takes special vows of service in the Church. In this paper, we follow the common usage. A nun is considered a religious and not a lay person. Lay persons are people who have not made special vows or promises of service to the Catholic Church. Also, in this paper "male religious" includes the three or four men who are diocesan priests and who therefore do not belong to religious orders or congregations. Technically, they are not religious, but in this paper, because their number is small, we group them with the men belonging to religious orders or congregations.

3. *The American College President* (Washington: American Council on Education Center for Policy Analysis, 2002). Hereafter cited simply as ACE 2001.

4. The Leadership Trends Study (LTS) data were coded using traditional methods of hand coding for qualitative data, and certain key questions were tracked on a percentage basis. All this information, along with written summaries, was given to the rest of the research team, who helped clarify findings, test assumptions, and hone the final results. In addition to the authors of this paper, three researchers participated in the project: Paul Gallagher is the former associate director and acting executive director of the Association of Catholic Colleges and Universities. He is presently a senior search consultant for R.H. Perry and Associates and brings a career of close relationships with presidents and the experience of coordinating their national conversations and concerns. Rev. John Piderit is the president of the Catholic Education Institute, past-president of Loyola University Chicago, and a Princeton-trained economist. Dr. Mary Lou Jackson had a seventeen-year career in administration at Stonehill College and recently received her Ph.D. from Boston College. Her dissertation focused on women and leadership in Catholic higher education. Their hard work and support was invaluable, and the study is far better for their challenging insights.

5. ACE 2001, Appendix B, 68. The ACE data are likely an inflated comparison in that they include presidents of divinity schools, whereas the LTS data exclude such institutions.

6. ACE 2001, Appendix B, 68.

7. ACE 2001, Appendix B, 64.

8. One caveat should be noted. Because priests, nuns, and brothers are religious professionals, the religious inspirations, aspirations and motivations that animate them in considering a presidency might well be considered their own unique kind of professional consideration.

9. Andrew M. Greeley, *From Backwater to Mainstream: A Profile of Catholic Higher Education* (New York: McGraw-Hill, 1969), 39. This number includes junior colleges, as well as four-year colleges. At times, women leaders operated under the title of "dean" with an honorary title going to a local bishop or his delegate as "president." For all intents and purposes, day-to-day leadership was always in the hands of women religious.

10. For purposes of this study, Carnegie category definitions have been used.

11. This represent a decrease from the 9.5% reported in 1998.

12. The University of San Diego is the Catholic doctoral-granting university that has a lay woman president, Dr. Alice Hayes. Upon her retirement, she will be succeeded by another lay woman, Dr. Mary Lyons, former president of the College of St. Benedict (in St. Joseph, Minnesota).

13. The names of the institutions and their new presidents are reported regularly by the Association of Catholic Colleges and Universities (ACCU) in their newsletter. For the names of presidents appointed over the last two years see, "Update," *ACCU Newsletter* 24 (4) through 31 (2).

14. The only sector of Catholic higher education in which women dominate as presidents is Catholic women's colleges. All the Catholic women's colleges, save one, have women presidents. Stephen J. Sweeny, the president of the College of New Rochelle, is the one male president of a Catholic college for women.

15. Finalist pool is an imprecise term. It is used here as respondents used it. In fact, respondents may have been referring to the group of people given serious consideration by trustees, not an official group of finalists.

16. It should be noted that Catholic colleges are not the only ones to counter this general trend. In one recent example, Princeton University's board of trustees, in selecting Shirley Tilghman as president, decided that academic and research credentials trumped administrative experience in terms of meeting the university's leadership needs.

17. Patricia Wittberg, "Reciprocal Identities: Apostolic Life and Consecrated Life," *Review for Religious* 61 (2002): 343.

18. In his book, *Liberal Arts Colleges: Thriving, Surviving, or Endangered?* (Washington: The Brookings Institution, 1994), David Breneman points out, "The experience of higher education in the 1980s has deviated strikingly from the pattern forecast by economists and other analysts in the late 1970s. Rarely has a body of predictions been so wrong" (2).

19. Breneman, *Liberal Arts Colleges*, 137.

Response to Morey and Holtschneider

JOHN J. DEGIOIA

Over the course of the last century there were a number of important moments in higher education when a document was produced that forever after defined the shape of conversation and discourse around a field. In particular, I am thinking of the earlier part of the twentieth century, when Abraham Plexner studied American medical schools, the mid-1940s, when Harvard produced its Red Book, and the late 1940s, when Vanover Bush did his study of the role of science in the context of university research and university education. And there are more recent documents that we are all familiar with from the 1980s. Catholic higher education is a work-in-progress, and we are seeing the first pass at some new research. I think that from now on our work is going to be defined by the kinds of findings in the research of Melanie Morey and Dennis Holtschneider.

I will reflect on three findings in the Morey and Holtschneider report that have led me to grasp a core conflict that I think we all wrestle with in the work of promoting Catholic identity. I hope that through these reflections I can help push us a little further to understand what is really at stake: the responsibility we all share in sustaining the Catholic identity of our institutions. The core conflict is this: Can we compete as an academy, as a college or university, in the American context and sustain an authentically Catholic character? Regardless of the context in which one is competing, can we compete as an academy and sustain an authentically Catholic character?

First, do lay leaders have the same legitimacy as religious leaders in the stewardship of Catholic universities? The work of promoting Catholic identity is the work of a community. It is not the sole responsibility of a president or a mission director. It is the responsibility of an entire community and sometimes of what the report refers to as an iconic figure. If we had one, we would never let him or her go! But on the other hand, the presence of an iconic figure enables a community to avoid the real work that is the responsibility of everyone.

History is replete with examples of institutions, religious orders, and all sorts of organizations that were inspired by powerful, charismatic leaders. When those leaders left or died, the followers were left with the difficult task of sustaining the charism and identity of that mission and organization. If we can be clear that the work of identity is the work of a community, then the implications for promoting Catholic identity will take on a positive dynamic for all of us as we wrestle with it.

Second is the concern by many about the lack of a clear definition of Catholic identity—what it means to be Catholic. Although I can identify with this frustration, I do think it is a category mistake in the report. I believe the work of Catholic identity is the work of definition. It is not something separate from the community that can be handed to us. It is not something static that can be handed over from one leader to another. The work of Catholic identity is an ongoing organic, evolving process of trying to determine how a specific community at a specific point in time—looking at its resources, opportunities, and challenges—determines how best to draw from the diverse elements of the Catholic tradition in order to strengthen its ability to engage and sustain its Catholic identity.

I thought of a couple of examples while I was reflecting on this. At Georgetown, in recent years we have discovered some resources that have simply jelled. We did not know in advance that they would come together in the way that they did, but somehow they did. For example, in 1994 we established a Center for Muslim-Christian understanding. There is a similar center at the seminary in Hartford, Connecticut, but the one at Georgetown is the only one sponsored by a university. The Center is led by arguably the nation's leading Islamist, John Esposito. He has assembled a wonderful faculty and has done extraordinary work over the last decade. In the same context where he is working, the

Center for Contemporary Arab Studies has also flourished, although it has been at Georgetown for about three decades. Recently we were able to secure support to establish an academic chair in the study of Jewish civilization. Jane McCauliff, one of the world's leading experts on the Qur'an, arrived a few years ago and serves as dean of our college, and is involved in every major interreligious discussion. When we look at where Georgetown is today, with Dean McCauliff, John Esposito, the Wiesel Chair coming on line, as well as three Jewish chaplains and an imam, this combination of resources enables us to engage our Catholic tradition by emphasizing and bringing focus to interreligious understanding.

Because of these resources, we can offer to a student of a different faith tradition a sincere respect that we have for them and their faith tradition, which probably would not occur in an institution that did not have such a commitment. We can provide a foundation for students to learn to respect. Instead of saying that we want to be open to a diversity of students and faculty and staff because it is the law, we are motivated by the conviction of respect for each individual person, because he or she is loved and created by God. But there is no confusion that the Catholic tradition is privileged at Georgetown by virtue of the way we structure our curriculum, by the presence of certain kinds of people, by the ways in which we celebrate certain public events, including our baccalaureate with a liturgy. One of the rabbis I alluded to earlier is Rabbi Harold White. He has been a member of the university community at Georgetown since 1968. He claims that Georgetown has sent more people on to rabbinical school than any other college in the country. So although we privilege one tradition, if a student comes, then he or she is part of a community that is conversant in the language of faith, and takes the idea of a transcendent reality very seriously.

Many of us have volume two of *Examining the Catholic Intellectual Tradition*, which is the result of the work that Sacred Heart University has been engaged in for a number of years. In this university, the Catholic intellectual tradition has been given a focus, a privilege, an emphasis. This work helps to sustain a vocabulary, a syntax, a grammar, for an important kind of intellectual discourse that could otherwise be lost. And at Boston College, Father William Leahy and Father Joseph Appleyard and a number of their colleagues have just done an extraordinary job over the last year in developing a program on the Church in the twenty-first century. This provides a forum and resources to assist the Catholic community in transforming the current clerical sexual abuse crisis into an opportunity for renewal. They looked at the resources they had and they were able to pull those resources together in a way that enables them to make a contribution that almost no one else could do. And it is an exceptional service to all of us that they are doing so.

So the real issue is not about defining what Catholic identity in the abstract. Rather, our efforts would be better directed towards promoting communal cooperation and responsibility towards bringing people together with the resources and opportunities that we have.

A third reflection builds on the former one. The work of Catholic identity is the work of the community and to say that the faculty is an obstacle to this effort is to confuse the nature of the work. It is just another way of saying that the work is difficult. This leads back to the core concern: Can we compete in the contemporary academy and share in the responsibility of sustaining a tradition to be authentically Catholic? From a leadership perspective, I do not think any of us would have accepted our responsibilities if we did not share a conviction that there is no better way to live out our vocations than in the context of the Catholic community. Can we share this vision with the faculty in a way that enables them to participate fully as they wrestle with all the demands that come with being a faculty member competing in the contemporary academy? Yes. And faculty members who find it difficult to participate and resist are still part of our community; they are part of the world that we are a witness to and trying to address.

Our work is to determine in this moment what elements of our tradition can be effectively engaged in a way that enables us to ensure that we can sustain an authentic Catholic community. The work is the work of the community; the role of leadership is to present the work in ways that can be engaged by all the members of the community—even those who are resistant. I think the challenge to compete as an academy and sustain an identity as authentically Catholic is a responsibility we all share. It is difficult, daunting, and frustrating, but I do not think any of us can imagine a more important way to spend our lives.

Response to Morey and Holtschneider

MARILOU ELDRED

The study by Morey and Holtschneider has done a service not only to Catholic higher education, but all of American higher education. I suspect that there are several follow-up studies that could complement theirs, and I foresee some doctoral students continuing to advance the research that is begun here.

Although I was not surprised by many of the results of the study, there were a few points that caused me to question some conclusions drawn. I am the only one of the three respondents who has a religious background, that is, I was a religious sister before becoming a lay president of a Catholic college. My response flows from that dual perspective.

I was a member of the Sisters of Charity of the Blessed Virgin Mary (BVM) for ten years, from 1959-69. The BVMs are exclusively a teaching order, staffing many grade and high schools and two colleges: Clarke in Dubuque, Iowa, home of the order's mother house, and Mundelein in Chicago, which merged with Loyola University in 1991. My professional life in the community consisted of three years of teaching high school, three years as assistant academic dean at Mundelein, and a year of graduate school in between to earn a master's degree in student personnel administration. Immediately after leaving the congregation, I returned to New York University, where I had earned a master's, to begin a doctoral program in higher education administration, completing that in 1974.

As a student and administrator at Mundelein, I learned to appreciate the importance of a college for women, and particularly a Catholic college for women. I was fortunate to work with many strong women leaders, such as Sister Ann Ida Gannon. I learned that women could and did do everything; there was no "glass ceiling," no questioning of women's ability to lead, to make corporate decisions, to be the spokesperson for a college. Women were in charge, although all the top level positions at that time were held by women religious, not lay women.

After completing my doctoral work, I decided that Catholic women's colleges were the place where I wanted to devote my life in higher education. I was fortunate to work at the College of St. Catherine for eighteen years, and to hold many senior-level positions there. It was a situation where, as we know in Catholic education, if there was a need, I filled it. I am very grateful for that experience and opportunity. When I decided I might be ready to consider and be considered for a college presidency, I knew that my preference would be for a Catholic women's college.

With that bit of personal history, I will now turn to the paper and my response. With regard to many of the statistical and demographic characteristics of Catholic college lay presidents, I think I fit the mold. My degree is in education and I was a former academic vice president, although there were no members of the founding congregation in the finalist pool when I was selected to be president at Saint Mary's College.

But I would differ with the researchers in some of their comments about mission fit and Catholic identity as a lay president. I certainly include several courses in theology and philosophy among my undergraduate studies, which have assisted me in an intellectual understanding of those disciplines and their place in the curriculum of a Catholic college. But I also believe, as a former religious sister, that I have a good sense of the mission of a Catholic college without formal theological education beyond the undergraduate level. I am committed to leading my institution in pursuit and fulfillment of its Catholic mission. Without denying the importance and necessity of advanced theological education, I believe it is possible for leaders of Catholic colleges without a formal education to possess a level of knowledge of Catholic mission and identify sufficient to be the presidents of those institutions.

A significant finding of the research is the fact that there are many fewer women presidents of Catholic institutions than male presidents, both religious and lay. Furthermore, the number of women presidents is declining, as the number of women religious declines. Of course, that is not surprising, considering that the Church continues to be led by a male hierarchy and women still are not considered equal with regard to important leadership positions in the Church. That could take us down a very different path from the focus of this discussion and it is an issue of which we are well aware.

It is interesting to me that congregational loyalty, presumption of legitimacy, religious literacy, and religious formation are four factors that the authors speculate are reasons for selecting religious over lay presidents, even when the religious person may not have administrative background pertinent to assuming the presidency. I wonder which colleges have made that kind of selection and if they are among what could be described as conservative Catholic colleges; and if they would make the same choice again. I also wonder if those religious presidents enjoy their work, since it was noted that the vow of obedience may have come into play in the selection of these presidents. It seems to me that it is important for all colleges, regardless of how they would describe themselves, to select presidents who can truly engage in the job of the president; this includes both lay and religious presidents. The job is too challenging, too varied, and too wide-ranging to be foisted upon someone with little or no interest. I would worry about the success of the presidency and the institution in such a situation.

With regard to questions of mission and Catholic identity, I believe the authors make two immensely important points. They discuss the complexity of the president's responsibilities in such a way that mission fulfillment may become one more in a series of important issues to be considered by the president. So if the president does not have formal preparation in theology, it may be no worse than having limited preparation in student life or fund raising. Also, some respondents to the study noted the importance of mission preparation for Catholic higher education as a whole, but seemed to diminish its importance for their particular institution. It is difficult to know what that means. I think these points underscore the imperative of continuing discussion, with a goal of clarification of issues relating to Catholic identity and mission. The Association of Catholic Colleges and Universities (ACCU) offers a wonderful service, with its trustee workshops, annual meeting, and ongoing consultation that its president, Monika Hellwig, provides. At some point, however, it would be helpful if, as part of the preparation for a Catholic college presidency, there would be specific knowledge areas that candidates should have in their repertoire. A model might be the master's program at the University of St. Thomas in St. Paul, and perhaps other places, that helps to prepare student personnel professionals for working in Catholic colleges.

At Saint Mary's College, we have a vice president for mission, a position created when the governance of the college moved from the congregation to a lay board of trustees. The person should preferably be a member of the Congregation of Holy Cross, the sponsoring order of the college, and is to be appointed jointly by the presidents of the congregation and the college. The position title is a bit of a misnomer, since her responsibilities are really for the Catholic mission of the college, and not for the liberal arts or women's components of the mission. It is difficult for many faculty and staff to understand this position. I consciously work at keeping the position visible in decision-making, public college events, and hiring issues, among others. I would venture that at Saint Mary's, there is probably more affinity and support for the charism of the congregation than there is for the mission vice president of the college. Many people think that because we have this position, she is responsible for the Catholic mission, and other faculty and staff "don't have to worry about it." So, I am concerned about how to make the most of this position, and I hope there will be discussion about it.

Many of our faculty were hired years ago when there were many sisters teaching and working in the college. They were hired largely for their disciplinary expertise and little mention was made of the specific attention to the Catholic mission of the college, assuming that the sisters were taking care of that. In our time, however, as we hire new people, we are deliberate in talking about the mission of Saint Mary's and try to ascertain the fit between the potential faculty or staff person and the Catholic mission of the college, as well as the academic discipline, the support for women's education, and the usual hiring factors.

Although we continue to demonstrate outwardly our identity as a Catholic college with crucifixes in every office and classroom, prayer as a regular part of meetings and many classes, a curriculum requirement in religious studies, a Center for Spirituality and a vice president for mission, I worry that the Catholic identity is not necessarily a vital part of the fabric of all that we do at our college.

Finally, I would emphasize the importance of strong leadership from the board of trustees in all of these issues. The president takes direction from the board and if mission issues are not a clear priority at the top level, it will be even more difficult for the president to change a culture that may need changing. We are seeing a new generation of board leadership where the religious congregational members are in the minority and may hold few, if any, board leadership positions. This underscores again, the importance of the ACCU workshops for trustees.

I have seen many dedicated lay presidents of Catholic institutions. I suspect that all of us are passionate about what we are doing with and for our institutions. I also suspect that we worry about how well we are leading our institutions as Catholic colleges, not just colleges in the U.S. system of higher education. Together, I hope that we can find a few answers and also be open to new questions.

Response to Morey and Holtschneider

ALICE B. HAYES

The past few decades have been a time of transition in Catholic higher education, reflecting great changes in society. Since Vatican II, we have seen a significant reduction in the number of religious, a change in the role of women in the governance of higher education, and a change in the Church itself. The college presidents today are different people facing different challenges than when I was a student in the 1950s, when Catholic colleges and universities were owned and operated by religious. Looking around us at the products of those earlier colleges, we ask, "Did those nuns and priests and brothers do a good job of preparing Catholic professionals and leaders?" If they did, then today's challenges can be managed. If they did not, then perhaps we should not look to those days as models for the future.

The study by Dr. Morey and Father Holtschneider makes a valuable contribution to our understanding of Catholic higher education and our leadership needs for the future. Lay presidents have become the majority and they appear to be well-prepared, perhaps better-prepared than some of their religious peers in terms of administrative experience in higher education. We may wonder why boards of trustees entrust multimillion-dollar operations to candidates who do not have experience in university administration. Of the religious who became college presidents, over one-third (38%) did not come from an administrative post. Fifteen percent moved into the presidency directly from a faculty position, and 22% (nearly one quarter) of the religious presidents came from outside higher education. I think these are astonishing statistics.

At the University of San Diego we have had lay leadership for thirty-two years. But I have been a member of other Catholic university boards of trustees on four occasions when they had been either looking for a president or reviewing the statutes that govern selection of a president. Two of the four would only consider members of the founding congregation, even though they knew that this meant that the pool of candidates would be sharply limited and that they might not be able to get the experience in the leader they sought. The third board decided that they would be open to lay candidates, but it was clear that this would not be their preference. The fourth board was open to lay candidates, but it was an easy decision because they did not expect that there would be any candidates from the founding community. None of the chairmen of these boards wanted to be the one who transferred leadership to a lay person. One went so far as to say that they would get a member of the religious community even if the person was not fully qualified, in which case they would hire someone else to provide the real administration of the university. What my experience and this study show is that leadership of mission is perceived by boards as the most important qualification for a president, and that it is often believed that a member of the religious community will do a better job preserving the institution's religious identity than a lay person would do. The religious person not only understands the charism and educational philosophy of the founding community, but he or she is also spiritually inspired and committed to it, and is therefore, considered a better candidate for leadership of the mission.

The number of religious educators prepared and available to lead Catholic universities is diminishing, and we will need to rely more on lay people to carry on the mission of Catholic higher education. As chairs of search committees have learned, it is very difficult to let go of these blanket preferences. When the founding communities or diocese can no longer provide leadership, something is lost. But then we have to move on with what is possible for the future. For some colleges, a number of religious from the founding community or diocese will be available and qualified for leadership, but for others, that will not be likely.

A criterion that this study used to measure one's ability to lead the religious mission of a Catholic college or university was the president's spiritual preparation and formal study of theology.

Lay presidents typically have modest theological background and have not had the spiritual formation experience that religious have. This is not to say that they do not have deep spirituality or adequate understanding of the major teachings of the Church. Rather, the spirituality of lay presidents is formed and experienced in different ways than that of the religious, and their understanding of Church teachings is usually not at the intellectually sophisticated level of a theologian.

For example, in my experience of over forty-one years in higher education, I recognize that the spirituality and theological knowledge of a lay person is not the same as that of a religious. Despite thirty-three years at Jesuit universities, as close and committed as I was to the educational mission, I never felt a deep resonance with the *Spiritual Exercises* of St. Ignatius of Loyola. There is much that I valued and ideas such as "persons for others," "doing all for the greater glory of God," and "finding God in things" were very meaningful to me, but the Exercises are not the kind of spiritual devotion designed for women, wives, or mothers. Similarly, the required four theology and five philosophy courses I took as an undergraduate gave me some familiarity with the language of Catholicism and encyclicals and dogma, but I have no real authoritative knowledge. I feel closer to the spiritual outlook of the Religious of the Sacred Heart that animates the University of San Diego where I spent the past eight years. But I know that my spiritual formation and theological foundation is not the same as that of a member of the religious community. Yet, as Morey and Holtschneider were surprised to learn from other lay presidents, despite our limitations we do not feel ill-equipped to lead the religious mission of our universities. I feel that, with appropriate effort on my part, I can translate the mission and charism for our students, faculty, and staff. The legacy of our founders lives in the lives of lay people—our faculty and alumni and the people whose lives they influence.

The preparation that Morey and Holtschneider have measured is the preparation to be a religious, not preparation to be a university president. They observe that a religious is "granted moral credibility and leadership through the structure of vows or ordination." There is no doubt that this happens, but as we have learned in recent years, ordination no more assures the moral credibility of a priest than baptism does for a lay person. I do not think that it is necessary or appropriate to prepare for leadership of a Catholic university in the same way one would prepare to be a sister, brother, or priest.

What the president needs, it seems to me, is a good foundation in the teachings of the Church that should ordinarily have been acquired over a lifetime as a practicing Catholic, which is updated continuously by study about the Church and Catholic issues today. For example, I find it helpful to regularly read several publications such as *Origins,* which reports weekly on the teachings of the Pope, the bishops and current topics, and *Commonweal* and *Logos* for treatment of issues of contemporary Catholic life and higher education. And there are many other publications that presidents find helpful. The questions that the president has to answer are not deep theological issues calling for advanced study in theology. Rather, we will be asked to comment on a current issue that touches on the faith, or more typically on morals, or the use of a controversial textbook, or the performance of a questionable play, or exhibition of a work of art, or a gay/lesbian or pro-choice guest speaker, or to approve a course or program for the curriculum. For this we need to understand Church teaching and know enough theology and philosophy to be able to read current Catholic literature on Church teaching on these education-related issues, or frame the question for a response by a trained theologian.

We also need formation programs that would thoroughly inform lay leaders of the history, charism, traditions, and educational philosophy of our particular founding congregations or dioceses. These programs should be made available to members of the board as well as the senior administrator's faculty.

The lay person will not be able to marry, bury, baptize, or spiritually counsel members of the university community and their families, and will not preside at Eucharistic liturgies, but should be able to lead the mission of the university. Founding communities should also be sensitive to the needs of the institutions they developed and if there are members of the community with an interest and ability in university leadership, they should see to it that these individuals get the administrative experience and training that they need to be effective in the universities they will serve. Both aspects of preparation—for leading the mission and for leading the university—are important.

There are several other issues raised by the Holtschneider and Morey study that deserve more attention than I can give them. I am not sure how to respond to the finding that the number of women leaders of Catholic colleges and universities is diminishing, but I suspect that this may be in part a consequence of the merger of women's colleges with men's colleges which then continue under their original and usually male leadership.

Another important observation was the recognition that lay college presidents desire but do not achieve working relationships with the hierarchical Church as easily as their religious peers. The authors suggest that there are more "informal conversations of leadership between bishop and college president in the comfort and context of shared religious profession." However, I think that the hierarchical authority relationship between bishop and religious may be a greater inhibitor of free exchange of views than the teaching authority relationship between bishop and lay president. The bishop and college president are obliged by *Ex Corde Ecclesiae* to develop a dialogue, and I that think we can do without tension.

The concern about lack of support for mission from faculty members is widespread. This study shows that most presidents believe that faculty development for mission is the real area of concern and one that must be addressed. All of us, whether religious or lay presidents, will need to focus on hiring for mission, orientation of new faculty, and faculty development programs for current faculty as we guide our institutions faithfully and fearlessly into the future.

PART II

Theological and Ecclesiological Foundations for Lay Leadership

Sent Out to Serve: Disciples of Jesus as Leaders of Catholic Colleges and Universities in a New Era

ANTHONY J. CERNERA

Dr. Morey and Father Holtschnieder have described in their study the changed reality of the composition of those who lead Catholic colleges and universities in the United States. Today, Catholic institutions of higher education draw their leaders overwhelmingly from the ranks of women and men whose full membership in the Church is defined by the Sacraments of Baptism, Confirmation, and Eucharist. The numbers of those in positions of leadership who also have received the Sacrament of Orders and/or who have professed vows within religious communities have declined significantly and will probably continue to do so. This is a dramatic historical change in a very short period of time. We find ourselves in a new place, a place that is exciting to many and frightening to others. This phenomenon of our times has great significance and consequences for those of us who are responsible for the mission and purposes of Catholic colleges and universities in the United States. It is also representative of a significant sign of the times that is broader than the higher education sector, namely the dramatic increase in the number of fully initiated members of the Christian community who are not ordained or professed religious but who are active and engaged participants in the mission and life of the Church. This extraordinary development reflects the reemergence of an ecclesial self-understanding that affirms the responsibility of all fully initiated members of the Church for the continuing mission of Christ in the world. The higher education phenomenon, and indeed the larger sign of the times that it illustrates, represents a major paradigm shift for the Christian community in every particular church around the world, one whose consequences we are still seeking to understand and to build on for the future.

This paradigm shift is also taking place within the American context and experience, which is a way of life that values participation. Participation is indeed a defining characteristic of our society and is informed by such values as equal opportunity, free expression, responsible citizenship, democratic process, and volunteerism. These values and others like them create and maintain a culture that fosters and encourages active engagement. In addition, Catholics in the United States have embraced the ideal of participation at many levels of church life. It is common practice to see members of the church who are not ordained or members of religious communities engaged in all kinds of ministries and various forms of activity within the community and beyond.

In addition, we are a church that is now in the mainstream of American society. From the middle of the nineteenth century until the late 1920s, the Catholic Church in the United States was an immigrant church. That began to change in the third decade of the twentieth century as Catholics gradually moved out of the immigrant ghettos of major cities, poverty, and the working class. Post-World War II America saw Catholics go to college in unprecedented numbers. The election of John F. Kennedy in 1960 marked a symbolic arrival of Catholics in the mainstream of American life. While no other Catholic has been elected president of the United States since that time, Catholics have come to occupy positions of leadership in corporate, civic, and public life that would have been unimaginable to the Catholic community a century and a half before.

An Autobiographical/Narrative Theology Excursion

Allow me a moment of autobiographical reflection to illustrate the paradigm shift. In 1967, I was a junior at Mount St. Michael's Academy, a wonderful high school for boys at which virtually all the teachers were members of the Marist Brothers of the Schools. My high school years, 1964 to 1968, proved a fascinating time to be studying and growing in my understanding of being a Christian. A group of young Marist Brothers freshly out of college had joined an already vibrant community of teachers. I was invited to join a student organization known as Young Christian Students (YCS) and to participate in a leadership development program. In religion class I was learning that all of us as baptized people were members of the Church. In fact, we were the Church: the people of God called to continue the mission of Christ in the world.

That was wonderfully exciting. It made perfectly good sense, capturing for me in words what I was experiencing when I was involved in a variety of activities that today would be called service learning. Along with others my age, we were teaching the gospel to young children. We were feeding the hungry at a soup kitchen. We were active in movements promoting peace, ecumenism, and the rights of oppressed people. And we were doing these kinds of things because we understood ourselves to be disciples of Jesus and a community of disciples of Jesus. We worked alongside priests, religious brothers and sisters, and occasionally even a bishop or two.

But all that said, it was also somewhat confusing to this then-young teenager. Confusing? Yes, because the community of Jesus' disciples was also trying to catch up with this and other developments in the life of the Church in the years immediately following the Second Vatican Council. Upon joining YCS, I was given some material about this wonderful movement, which had been written just before the Council. In that printed material, our work of bringing the gospel into the social setting of our world was described as "participating in the work of the hierarchy." Somehow by joining YCS or the Sodality or some other Catholic youth organization we were taking on a work that was not properly ours but belonged to the bishops. A few of us "lay people" were invited to share in what was really the work of the bishop. That sounded very different from what I was learning and what I was experiencing. So my confusion amounted to answering the apparent contradiction: Was I responding to the gospel in the ways that I was because I was a baptized member of the Church, or was I called and chosen to assist in the work of the ordained leaders of the diocese or parish? Was I the Church, along with all the other baptized members, or were the ordained really the Church in which I had some minor but finally insignificant role?

The confusion of that time was expressed in another way in my personal journey of discipleship. I was considered a prime candidate for religious life or for ordination. According to some people, Tony was "holy" and active in various charitable works, so it was presumed that I was being called to religious life or priesthood. But that was not how I was experiencing it. On the other hand, there were few role models out there of people who were trying to be "holy" and active in following Jesus' way that were not ordained or professed religious. So I was confused. People I respected greatly thought I should enter a particular religious community or the diocesan seminary. I decided that I should make a retreat. And so I did. In fact, I went on retreat three times during a six-year period and each time the message was clear: I was not called to those ways of discipleship. Rather, I was called to live as a disciple of Jesus, fully as a member of the church, trying to give my life fully to God just as I am.

Perhaps that was more than you want to know about me, but it may help to set the stage for a theologically informed reflection about those of us who are called from the community to be leaders of Catholic colleges and universities in a new era of church and society.

So we are at a very different place in the life of the church and the life of Catholic universities and colleges. We are seeking ways to understand ourselves, and to be understood by others in the church. We are full members of the church by virtue of the sacraments of initiation and we are also leaders who live their professional lives as an integral part of their vocation to respond to the saving love that God has revealed to us in Jesus of Nazareth. This is a dramatically new development, and the church's effort to reflect on this profound paradigm shift is still very tentative. Over the last thousand years, the church has paid little attention to the role of those whose lives were not characterized by ordination or religious profession. Most of us have become accustomed to mean the ordained when we say "church." We have divided the church into "clerical" and "lay" in ways that nurtured an ideal of being a good lay Catholic that was about obedience and passivity and hardly about active, full, conscious participation in and responsibility for the mission of the church. It was understood that the ones who did that kind of work were the priests and nuns.

When it comes to our colleges and universities, the issues play themselves out much the same way. For example, I have been asked at least a thousand times: Which religious order founded Sacred Heart University or which group of priests or nuns runs the university? It is always interesting to watch the expression on peoples' faces when I say that the responsibility for the founding and leading of this University has been and continues to be in the hands of a group of men and women who are active members of the church, and who are also spouses and parents.

My task in this essay is to offer a theological reflection about who we are as full members of the Church who are also called to be leaders of Catholic colleges and universities at the beginning of the twenty-first century in the United States. I propose to undertake this reflection by: 1) describing some of the key themes of the Second Vatican Council; 2) focusing on the mission and ministry of Jesus and his disciples; 3) suggesting a way of understanding ourselves as disciples who lead Catholic colleges and universities; and 4) concluding with some challenges for us to address in the years ahead.

The Second Vatican Council: The Call for *Aggiornamento* and Reading the Signs of the Times

The most important event in the life of the Roman Catholic Church in the twentieth century was the Second Vatican Council. This is the case for several reasons. First, it was the first time in the life of the community of Jesus' disciples that the world church met. The phrase "world church" was first used by Walbert Buhlmann and adopted by Karl Rahner to capture a radical new development in the life of the Catholic Church. Although there had been ecumenical councils before in the history of the church, this was the first time that bishops came from every continent, and those bishops included men who were native to those geographical areas. The community of Jesus' disciples was exhibiting its Catholicity in a universal and global way. Among the bishops from Asia there were Asians; among those from Africa there were Africans—and not merely European and American missionaries who had become bishops of churches on that continent. And the same was true of the bishops who came from Latin America. This was reflective of a profound change in the face and composition of the Christian community worldwide. For the first time in its two-thousand-year history there were more Catholics from outside Europe and North America, a trend that would continue in a dramatic way well into the twenty-first century.

Second, by convening the Council, Pope John XXIII invited the church into a profound examination about its inner life (*ad intra*) and its relationship to the world (*ad extra*). He further asked that it be done in a spirit of profound faith and confidence in what God was doing in history, and not in a posture of defensive condemnation. At the ceremonies on the opening day of the Council, Pope John XXIII said:

> In the daily exercise of our pastoral ministry—and much to our sorrow—we must sometimes listen to those who, consumed with zeal, have scant judgment or balance. To such ones the modern world is nothing but betrayal and ruin. They claim that this age is far worse than previous ages, and they rant on as if they had learned nothing at all from history—and yet, history is the great Teacher of Life. . . . We feel bound to disagree with these prophets of doom who are forever forecasting calamity—as though the world's end were imminent. Today, rather, Providence is guiding us toward a new order of human relationships, which, thanks to human effort and yet far surpassing human hopes, will bring us to the realization of still higher and undreamed of expectations.[1]

Third, the Council was both the culmination of a long process of self-reflection and preparation for renewal as well as the point of departure for a more intense effort at renewal and updating on the part of the church in response to a radically changing world. The Council stood as a watershed point, but the work of the Council needed to be received and incorporated into the life of the

Church. For example, the renewal of the liturgy, which called for the "full, conscious, and active participation in liturgical celebrations,"[2] represented the culmination of a century of preparation by liturgical scholars, many of them Benedictine monks in Europe. The same could be said for the biblical movement that prepared the way for the revival of biblical studies in the Catholic community as well as the recovery of the sacred Scriptures as an integral part of Catholic worship and daily spiritual life and practice (*lectio divina*). However, the Council also broke significant new ground in its teaching on religious liberty, ecumenical relations with other Christian churches, inter-religious dialogue, indeed in the church's very understanding of its relationship to the world. The Council invited the church to engage in a new way of theological reflection about its mission in the world by positing the starting point for such reflection in the reading of the signs of the times. The Council acknowledged that the Church had something to learn from the world because God's Spirit was actively engaged in the great events of history, calling the Church and all people of good will to participate in renewing the face of the earth.

Fourth, for our purposes, the most critical development at the Council was the Church's reflection on its own self-understanding. The *aggiornamento* that the Council undertook brought the church to a new self-definition. As Hermann J. Pottmeyer wrote:

> The critical impulse that can be seen at work during and after the Council was aroused because the official self-understanding of the Church which right up to the Council had been formed by a counter-reformational and neo-scholastic theology, had become questionable. It had become increasingly alien to the real life of human beings and no longer met the needs of an effective pastoral practice.[3]

The pre-Vatican II definition was overly juridical and excessively clerical. For example, take the definition of the church of Robert Bellarmine that was commonly used in pre-conciliar times, namely, "The one and true Church is the community of men brought together by the profession of the same Christian faith and conjoined in the communion of the same sacraments, under the government of the legitimate pastors and especially the one vicar of Christ on earth, the Roman pontiff." The Council, after rejecting an initial schema on the Church in which the first chapter was entitled "The Nature of the Church Militant," adopted as the title of its first chapter, "The Mystery of the Church." As Avery Dulles pointed out in his classic work, *Models of the Church*, "This change was symptomatic of the whole ecclesiology of the Council"[4] By doing this, the Council refocused the church on what is most important about itself, namely, the presence of God in it, who calls the members to life with God, sustains them, and works through them to bring about the fulfillment of the Reign of God. This change led initially to the theological reflection of the church as "People of God" as the Council's preferred way of describing the church. Gradually at the Council and afterwards, the notion of *communio* also emerged. The Extraordinary Synod of 1985 concluded its written reflection this way: "The ecclesiology of communion is the central and fundamental idea of the Council's documents." Georgia Keightley reminds us that *communion,* like its Greek equivalent *koinonia,* "is an ancient one, and unlike the images found in *Lumen Gentium* that merely describe the Church, this word says what the Church actually is."[5] *Koinonia* is a central New Testament term. She continues:

> It has as referents both God's grace and the human response to it. Primarily, it is used to express the understanding early Christians had of themselves as constituting an entirely new form of human community, a society whose very principle of unity and identity was the felt presence of God's own self. This shared experience of union with God through Christ in the Spirit was not only the basis for the union between believer and believer and source of the local Church's common life, it was also recognized to be the bond that linked the local Church to Christian communities everywhere, past as well as present.

A fundamental practical consequence of this new self-understanding was the rediscovery of the 99% of the Christian community who are baptized persons responding to the call of the Lord and living their lives of discipleship in the world and in the church. It is by virtue of three sacraments of initiation that all members of the Church participate as co-equal members of the People of God. As H. Richard McCord notes:

> Equality comes from the Sacrament of Baptism which, along with Confirmation and the Eucharist, joins all to Christ. By reason of this sacramental union, the People of God receive the gifts of the Spirit (charisms) enabling them to participate in the priestly, prophetic, and kingly mission of Christ. All differences and distinctions among the People of God are secondary in view of the fundamental unity they share as a "royal priesthood" derived from their baptism.[6]

In addition, all members of the Church were called to holiness, not just a select few. However, not only their dignity as full members of the Church, but also the warrant for all members of the Church to participate in the mission of the Church is given to all the members of the Church because they have been united to Christ in the sacraments of initiation—Baptism, Confirmation, and Eucharist. The apostolate of those fully initiated into the Body of Christ is "a participation in the saving mission of the Church itself. Through their baptism and confirmation, all are commissioned to that apostolate by the Lord Himself."[7] All members of the Church are fully constituted *christifideles*, and as such, they participate in Christ's three-fold mission of priest, prophet, and king. The mission of the Church itself and of all its members has its origin and foundation in the mission of Jesus.

The Mission and Ministry of Jesus

The mission of Jesus is critical for any understanding of Christian mission and ministry. All Christian mission and ministry are centered in the mission and ministry of Jesus. He is the primordial sacrament of the church's mission and ministry, without whom there would be no vocation for individuals in the church. What was Jesus about? From this we can then reflect on what it means to be a disciple of Jesus, particularly a disciple of Jesus who is called upon to lead a Catholic college or university in the United States today.

If we turn to the earliest of the four Gospels, that of St. Mark, we find Jesus at the outset of his public ministry proclaiming his central message: "The time has come and the kingdom of God is close at hand. Repent and believe the Good News" (Mark 1:14-15). He is sent by the Father to proclaim the in-breaking and the nearness of the kingdom of God and on the basis of this to invite those who hear this proclamation to repent and to believe the Good News. In her wonderful book, *Consider Jesus*, Elizabeth Johnson describes the Reign of God this way:

> Taken from the Hebrew tradition this symbol [the "reign of God"] signifies what the state of affairs will be when God is recognized as the One on whom everyone sets their hearts, when God finally reigns. The kingdom of God is God getting the divine way unopposed by human sinfulness and the powers of darkness. . . . The reign of God is the situation that results when God's will is really done.[8]

In response to the preaching of the Reign of God, we are invited to repent and to believe the Good News. The word so often and so misleadingly translated as "repent" is *metanoiete.* This Greek term is based on two words, *meta* (beyond) and *nous* (mind or spirit) and thus, in its most basic form, it means something like "go beyond the mind that you have." Jesus is urging his listeners first and foremost to change their way of knowing, their way of perceiving and grasping reality, their perspective, their mode of seeing. What Jesus is suggesting is that the Reign of God is here, right in our midst, waiting to break in now, if we only would open our eyes to see and then act accordingly, that is, act in a way that is consistent with the way that God intends. And what does God want? Johnson puts it simply and beautifully: "God wills our well being. God wants the wholeness, the healing and salvation of every creature and of all of us taken together."[9]

Jesus' message is also an invitation to believe the Good News. For Jesus this has far more to do with being known than as a way of knowing. To have faith is to open oneself to the gift of God's very self, to be overwhelmed by the power of God's unconditional love for us, and to let that Love reign at all levels of our being. As such, it is not primarily a matter of understanding and assenting to propositions as it is surrendering to the God who wants to be incarnate in us. In Paul Tillich's famous phrase, "Faith is being grasped by Ultimate Concern." Hence when Jesus urges his listeners to believe, he is inviting them and us to let go of the dominating and fearful ego within us and to learn to live our lives at the true center of our being, God's unconditional love for us.

As the gospel narrative unfolds, St. Mark brings us to the central questions: "Who do you say that I am?" (Mark 8:29). Peter gives the correct answer, "You are the Christ" (Mark 8:29). However, Jesus must explain what it means to be the Christ. In so doing, he describes what it means to be a leader and a disciple in his community. Peter understandably was anticipating a messiah who would lead Israel to prominence and power. Jesus startles his disciples with a radically different message about what it meant to be the messiah, an understanding that would challenge the conventional understanding to the core.

According to Mark:

> And he began to teach them that the Son of Man was destined to suffer grievously, to be rejected by the elders and the chief priests and the scribes, and to be put to death, and after three days to rise again; and he said of this quite openly. (Mark 8:31-32)

Jesus does not stop there, however. What is true of the messiah will also be true for the followers of the Anointed One:

> If anyone wants to be a follower of mine, let him renounce himself and take up his cross and follow me. For anyone who wants to save his life will lose it; but

> anyone who loses his life for my sake, and for the sake of the Gospel will save it. (Mark 8:34-39)

Even the followers of Jesus completely misunderstand what Jesus was teaching about the messiah, discipleship, and being a leader in the new community of Jesus followers, as illustrated in Mark 10:37-45:

> [James and John, the sons of Zebedee came forward and said to Jesus,] "Grant us to sit, one at your right hand and one at your left, in your glory." But Jesus said to them, "You do not know what you are asking. Are you able to drink the cup that I drink, or be baptized with the baptism with which I am baptized? And they said to him, "We are able." And Jesus said to them, "The cup that I drink you will drink; and the baptism with which I am baptized, you will be baptized; but to sit at my right hand or at my left is not mine to grant, but it is for those for whom it has been prepared." And when the ten heard it, they began to be indignant at James and John. And Jesus called them to him and said, "You know that those who rule over the Gentiles lord it over them, and their great men exercise authority over them. But it shall not be so among you. Whoever would be great among you must be your servant, and whoever would be first among you must be the slave of all. For the Son of Man also came not to be served but to serve, and to give his life as a ransom for many.

Saint Paul captured the same theme earlier when he quoted a very early Christian hymn in his letter to the Philippians 2:6-11:

> Christ Jesus, though he was in the form of God, did not count equality with God, a thing to be grasped, but emptied himself, taking the form of a servant, being born in the likeness of humans. And being found in human form, he humbled himself and became obedient unto death, even death on a cross. Therefore, God has highly

> exalted him and bestowed on him the name which is above every other name, so that at the name of Jesus, every knee must bow, in heaven, on the earth and under the earth, and every tongue proclaim that Jesus Christ is Lord, to the glory of God the Father.

Put simply, the paradigm for us as followers of Jesus is the Paschal Mystery. Jesus invites his disciples to be willing and ready to die to an old way of life of sin, power, and slavery, and to rise to live as he lives in the power of the Holy Spirit who brings life out of death and who draws all of us into the great harvest of justice and peace, God's reign among us.

Eucharist as a Way of Understanding Ourselves as Disciples Who Lead Catholic Colleges and Universities

It is interesting to remember that the Christian community has celebrated this Paschal Mystery from its earliest days as Eucharist. In St. John's Gospel, Jesus asked his disciples to "do this is remembrance of me." In the earlier writings of St. Paul, we hear: "On the night . . . Jesus, the Servant of God, who is the Paschal Victim and Victor is Eucharist." So perhaps leadership in the Christian community is also about being Eucharist. What do I mean? When the community of Jesus' disciples celebrates the Eucharist, the actions involved are: 1) being called together; 2) giving a blessing; 3) breaking bread; 4) sharing the broken bread and the cup of salvation; and 5) being sent forth. So the key actions—called, blessed, broken, shared, and sent—perhaps give us a way of understanding who we are as Jesus' disciples and as leaders of Catholic colleges and universities.

Called

In the sacraments of initiation each and every one of us has been called to carry on the mission of Jesus in the world today. We are invited to take seriously that God has called (and continues to call) each of us to do a particular work as God's partner along with other disciples and people of good will. This challenges us to develop the spiritual discipline to listen to the voice of God calling us in the ordinary circumstances of our lives as educators and administrators. Outrageous? Perhaps! But it is how God acts.

Blessed

Each and every one of us is a gift of God, and as a gift we are blessed and a blessing. The one who leads in the spirit of Eucharist humbly accepts his or her life as blessing with the full recognition that that gift he or she is and the gifts and talents he or she possess have been given freely by God.

Broken

The one who leads in the spirit of the Eucharist is deeply aware that Jesus was broken and that his dying and rising is the pattern of life for all those who follow in his way. The one who leads accepts the invitation to be open, to be vulnerable, to risk experiencing rejection and suffering. He or she can expect no more than the promise made to Peter by Jesus in the last chapter of John's Gospel. After Jesus asked Peter three times if he loved him, and Peter responded "yes," Jesus said to Peter, "feed my lambs," "tend my sheep," and then again, "feed my sheep" (John 21:15-17). Jesus continues:

> Truly, truly, I say to you, when you were young, you girded yourself and walked where you would; but when you are old, you will stretch out your hands, and another will gird you and carry you where you do not wish to go. (John 21:18)

Shared

The bread that is broken and the cup of salvation at the Eucharist must be shared. The one who leads in this way must be willing to share who he or she is and the blessings that each has been given with others, especially the poor and disadvantaged. This aspect of our leadership will challenge us deeply.

Sent

The community that is gathered by God's call is always sent. We are being sent out in this era to do something new as leaders of Catholic colleges and universities. We draw from a source of commissioning that comes from our baptism and we engage in a work that is our responsibility by virtue of our membership in the Church. We remain in communion with those leaders in the Church whose mission and ministry are defined differently than ours because of their ordination and/or religious profession.

Conclusion

By way of conclusion, let me dwell for several moments on the characteristic of being sent. Being sent is almost never easy. It often suggests going to unknown places and the unknown can be very frightening. The first disciples of Jesus were sent out by him to bring the Good News to the ends of the earth. For most of them that meant going to places that they had never been to before and to engage people who were very different then them. They often had to learn new languages and ways of interacting. From earliest days, they were faced with issues that were new and challenged them to think and act differently from the ways their known experience and culture would have suggested.

Recall some of the issues facing them:

- What should we do when the first non-Jews want to join the community of disciples and live according to the gospel?
- What should we do when it is no longer possible to remain members of the synagogue?
- How should we present the good news about Jesus and reflect on who one is?
- Who is the God that is revealed in Jesus in language that would make at least some sense to Greeks and Romans?
- How should the community of disciples relate to the Roman Empire?

- How should the community organize itself once it is separated from the Jewish community?

And these are only some of the issues.

Today we are also being sent. We are creating models of leadership for Catholic colleges and universities that are led by members of the church who are not ordained or members of religious communities. This is new for the church. The incorporation of the understanding of church that includes all fully initiated members into the life of the church is still going on, and frankly, is being resisted by some who would prefer to go back to the pre-conciliar era's understanding of the church. Part of our task is to assist in the ongoing reception and incorporation of the ecclesial self-understanding that was developed at the Council. This suggests several things.

First, at the programmatic level within and between our institutions, this means that we need to develop and foster programs of ongoing theological education as well as programs of spiritual development and renewal for the leaders of our colleges and universities. Second, it also suggests the importance of leadership development programs for students on our campuses who feel called to professional lives of service as leaders of Catholic colleges and universities. Third, there is a real need for ongoing dialogue with bishops at the local and national levels so that the truth of who we are as church will be developed and continually renewed. However, the challenges that we face are not only for the church. The emergence of fully initiated members of the church in positions of leadership is occurring at a time of profound transition and even in some respects crisis. This is true for American society, the higher education within our society, and for the Catholic Church in the United States.

As a civil society we are still feeling the after-shocks of the tragedy of September 11, 2001, and the factors that caused it. This has challenged us as a people to redefine ourselves and our place in the world. What does it mean to be an American? What in our way of life needs to be examined and purified as we seek to create a world of greater justice and peace? How do we reduce the reigning logic of instrumental reason which tends to reduce the dignity and worth of each human being to an economic factor? How do we foster a genuine sense of human solidarity that is respectful of the dignity and worth of every human being, cultivates a sense of global responsibility, and yet respects the unique expressions of various cultures and traditions?

As a part of the larger society, higher education is facing enormous challenges. The rise of for-profit universities and the emergence of technology within a customer-driven environment is challenging all of us to define our mission and become more efficient in our enterprise. In addition, significant numbers of colleges, especially smaller Catholic colleges that are not well endowed, struggle daily with the economics of survival in an environment that is increasingly complex and competitive.

Finally, we lead Catholic colleges and universities as members of a church that is deeply divided and in crisis, the immediate outcome of which is not at all clear. John T. McGreevy, in his recent book *Catholicism and American Freedom*, describes the present situation in the Church this way:

> The polarities are stark: on the one hand, an institution enrolling more active members than any other in American society, including prominent leaders in government, the professions, the universities, the trade unions and all branches of American industry. The same institution is important to the Latino community now taking center stage in American public life, and offers more social services, including soup kitchens, schools, hospitals, and community organizing projects, than any other organization besides the federal government. On the other hand, a wounded, fractious church, ripped apart by disputes over sex, gender, and ministry, and incapable of sustaining the loyalty of many of its communicants.[10]

These challenges within the society, within higher education generally, and within the Church require us to continue to engage in the kind of reflection that *Gaudium et Spes* invited the church to when it developed the methodology of reading the signs of the times in the light of the gospel. This is a continuing and ongoing task. Our task as leaders is to foster this way of reflection as critical to our mission as Catholic colleges and universities.

Our task is enormously important and difficult. We need to find the ways to support one another as we seek to respond to our call to be leaders, and as we journey in this new land to which we have been sent, we will need to reflect carefully on our experience, articulate a theology from that experience in the light of the gospel, learn from our mistakes, and remain deeply rooted in God, who raised Jesus the Christ from the dead. And yet, our task is also an enormous blessing. We have the opportunity to assist the community of Jesus' disciples in its ongoing mission and renewal and by so doing help in repairing the world into that garden of justice and peace that is the Reign of God among us.

Notes

1. Pope John XXIII, in *History of Vatican II, Volume II: The Formation of the Council's Identity, First Period and Intercession, October 1962–September 1963*, ed. Giuseppe Alberigo; English edition ed. Joseph A. Komonchak (Maryknoll, NY: Orbis/Peeters, 2001).

2. *Constitution on the Liturgy* [*Sacrosanctum Concilium*], #14, in Austin Flannery, ed., *Vatican Council II: The Conciliar and Post Conciliar Documents* (Wilmington, DE: Scholarly Resources, 1975).

3. Hermann J. Pottmeyer, "The Reception of Vatican II," in *The Reception of Vatican II*, ed. Giuseppe Alberigo, et al. (Washington: Catholic University of America Press, 1987), 30.

4. Avery Dulles, *Models of the Church*, 2nd edition (Dublin: Gill and MacMillan, 1988), 9.

5. Georgia Masters Keightley, "Vatican II: The Church's Self-Understanding," in Anthony J. Cernera, ed., *Vatican II: The Continuing Agenda* (Fairfield, CT: Sacred Heart University Press, 1997), 4

6. H. Richard McCord, "Full, Conscious, and Active Participation: The Laity's Quest," in *Vatican II: The Continuing Agenda*, 155.

7. *Dogmatic Constitution on the Church* [*Lumen Gentium*] (1964), #33, in Flannery, ed., *Vatican Council II: The Conciliar and Post Conciliar Documents.*

8. Elizabeth Johnson, *Consider Jesus: Waves of Renewal in Christology.* (New York: Crossroad, 1990), 51-52.

9. Johnson, *Consider Jesus*, 52.

10. John T. McGreevy, *Catholicism and American Freedom* (New York: W.W. Norton, 2003), 293.

Response to Anthony J. Cernera

JOHN E. THIEL

It may be helpful to the reader for me to summarize the argument of Anthony Cernera's paper briefly. In my response, though, I also would like to explore further some of the important issues that he addresses so well.

Cernera proposes an understanding of Christian discipleship derived from the words and deeds of Jesus, as well as from the fuller understanding of the Church taught at the Second Vatican Council. He catalogues all the ways in which the Second Vatican Council truly was a watershed in the age-old Catholic tradition. The Council was the first meeting of the "world church," the Church's entrée into a graceful globalization in a genuinely pluralistic way. The Council was characterized by a real openness to the Spirit, resisting the cynicism of some of its participants who could only see the sky falling in any prospect for change. The Council drew on recent movements in the Church in order to appreciate anew the holiness of its liturgy, the richness of its Scriptures, and the presence of God in every moment of history, not only in the secured past, but also in the ambiguous present and anticipated future. Most important for his argument, Cernera locates the Council's signal achievement in its theology of the Church. This theology filled out the largely institutional understanding of the Church in place since the sixteenth century by attending to the Church as the entire People of God animated by God's own presence. This fuller understanding of the Church has enabled us to see the Church as all the faithful called to discipleship by their baptism. Whereas the earlier institutional model envisioned the Church largely in the visibility of its structures and its hierarchy, the Council's community model found the reality of the Church in the corporate responsibility of all believers to be fully engaged disciples of Jesus.

In exemplary Catholic fashion, Cernera reads scripture through the eyes of tradition, bringing the teaching of Vatican II to bear on the call of Jesus to discipleship. That call, Cernera argues, is not made to some but to all believers. Although we encounter and embrace that call as individuals to some degree, the true meaning and reality of discipleship is as social as the human world in which we live, which, as redeemed, takes shape as the social reality of the kingdom of God's love, about which Jesus spoke whenever he was able to gather an audience. Leadership and its authority in that community of discipleship should never be a matter of "lording over" but rather of humble service to others.

Cernera appeals to the Eucharist as a paradigm for discipleship, finding in the actions of its celebration keys for identifying both the responsibilities and consequences of discipleship. Again returning to Vatican II's theology of the Church, he insists that just as we are all called to discipleship in the mystery of our baptismal faith, so are we all sent into the world to engage it in the same faith, to preach Christ fearlessly by our words and deeds. This commission to spread the gospel message is one that all believers embrace where they stand. The documents of the Council refer to this situated-ness of the call to be a Christian as the "apostolate of like towards like."[1] Cernera asks us to consider the implications of this apostolate for our shared vocation as leaders in the mission of Catholic colleges and universities.

Such is my summary. Now I would like to consider Cernera's generous autobiographical remarks, since they tell us not only something about the past but also much about our present moment. Cernera recalls that as a high-school student in 1967, his call to a life of holiness clashed with the expectation of contemporaries that such a vocation could only be satisfied in priestly ministry, a vocation to which he was not called. He tells us that as a young man he was theologically educated. He knew that the Council had taught that "all the faithful enjoy a true equality with regard to the dignity and the activity which they share in the building up of the body of Christ" and that even "the distinction which the Lord has made between the sacred ministers and the rest of the people of God implies union."[2] And yet, although he knew this, the conflict caused a nagging confusion. He made three retreats in six years to confirm what he already knew but from he which felt pressured to expect something different. Confusion reigned as theological theory did not jibe very well with actual life in the Church.

Cernera's confusion was a function of his theological education. He was confused because he knew the Church's teaching about the reality of the Church and yet it did not match the lived reality of a Church often too comfortable with the notion that serious Christianity is only for those living a consecrated life.

Even more of us are confused today because even more of us are theologically educated. I think it fair to say this is true much more through the achievement of our Catholic colleges and universities than of our parish education programs. This confusion is at once wonderful and distressing. The doctrine of the Second Vatican Council, the teaching of the Church about the Church, is a wonderful thing to know. It is distressing because in many respects we find ourselves in much the same place that Cernera stood in 1967. A surprising number in the Church today remain uneducated about the equality of our vocation in baptism, and those who are thus educated continue to face the striking mismatch between the doctrine they know and the reality of ecclesial life in which they live. The circumstances of our current situation, however, are not exactly the same as they were in 1967.

The Church today is not animated by the spirit of optimism that filled it in 1967. Instead, it is filled with a palpable anxiety, much of it stirred by the lines drawn today between the hierarchy and the laity and focused on the integrity of the ministerial priesthood. This anxiety has been fueled by a precipitous drop in priestly vocations since the Council, by polls that show a majority of the faithful do not agree with the Magisterium's restriction of priestly ordination to men, and, most recently, the sex abuse crisis in the American Church. This anxiety often has the effect of emphasizing the difference between priestly vocation and the baptismal vocation of every Christian to a life of holiness in a way that misrepresents and sometimes even ignores the Church's authoritative teaching. Whereas the Council teaches that there is an authentic distinction between the laity and the hierarchy, the distortion of this teaching transforms legitimate difference into a vocational divide.

Why does this disjunction continue between the Church's teaching and the reality of life in the Church? No doubt there are many and complex answers to this question, but here I venture a single and simple one: because so many in the Church have a vested interest in the clerical/lay divide. The anxieties surrounding the ministerial priesthood that I described a moment ago are largely those of the hierarchy. Although these anxieties are understandable in an ambiguous age like our own, they, like any form of fear, often produce distorted results. A recent manifestation of these anxieties is a kind of narcissism about the priesthood that one finds especially in young priests, whose homilies are much more likely to be about their own priestly vocation, their last trip to Rome, or the seeming primacy of papal authority in the hierarchy of truths than about the immeasurable depths of God's love or the experience of grace in the day-to-day lives of their congregation. In an age of anxiety about the priesthood, there are perceived advantages, however wrong-headed, in promoting the integrity of the priesthood by stressing its utter vocational difference from the vocation of all believers.

The hierarchy, though, is by no means the only party at fault here. The abiding clerical/lay divide is powerfully fostered by many of the lay faithful, whether they are theologically educated or not. The responsibility of the baptismal vocation that Vatican II articulates so well is often regarded by the laity as an onerous task happily left to the professional clerics who have "signed on" for a job most would rather avoid. After all, leading a holy life, being a truly faithful disciple of Jesus, is an extraordinarily difficult thing to do, and so many lay faithful are relieved, quite frankly, to think that this is someone else's lot in life.

Perhaps it should not surprise us that the clerical/lay divide endures in all quarters of the contemporary Church, even though we are approaching the fortieth anniversary of the Council's close. If we are easy on ourselves, we will offer explanations such as "our tradition is old, and moves slowly, and it is taking us time truly to appreciate the teaching of the Council." I think that a better theological explanation would point to the different varieties of resistance to the Council's teaching as manifestations of sin. And since, as Catholics, we believe that sin is resistible with the aid of divine grace, there is no need for us as a Church to continue in our old ways but to work at making the clerical/lay divide into a doctrinally informed clerical/lay distinction, fully committed to the Christian vocation that we all share.

Any meaningful consideration of lay leadership in Catholic higher education, to say nothing of lay leadership in the Church at large, must begin with the theological foundations that Cernera has sketched for us, lest our understanding of leadership be fashioned by some other template out there in the world ready to be grasped as effective and expedient: public opinion, the bottom line, the drives of educational consumerism, and so forth. It is important that we understand our leadership to be a ministry, and so the expression of a charism, our theological way of describing talent energized by God's grace. Also, we should remember that charismatic ministries in all quarters of the Church are often salaried, directly or indirectly, and that no contradiction exists in that. It seems to me that all our talk about Catholic identity in our colleges and universities in recent years often proliferates in confusing ways precisely because we do not begin by attending to the ways in which our common vocation in baptism makes our educational mission a ministry that we should understand as humble service to the gospel.

It is difficult for us to think of leadership in this way for a host of reasons. The gospel is so challenging; other understandings of leadership, like those drawn from the corporate world, seem so much more practical, respected in our culture, and readily recognized by our trustees; and, as all of us know, colleges and universities are not typically places where the virtue of humility carries the day. But at the heart of our difficulty with ministerial leadership is the central point in Cernera's paper: the way that the clerical/lay divide makes ministry a living responsibility only for a small number of Catholics who occupy very few of the positions of leadership in Catholic education today. Our commitment to that divide means that we never even have to face the issue of what leadership conceived as ministry in service to the gospel might mean concretely in our lives as believers and in our lives as believers who carry on the mission of Catholic education.

I hope we can consider some of the first steps Cernera proposes to us in facing the responsibility of lay leadership: ongoing theological education, development programs for students called to the vocation of leadership in Catholic colleges and universities, and ongoing dialogue with bishops. In concluding, I would like to call attention to the advice that Cernera offers about how we should reflect on the responsibility of leadership and its practical implementation.

I appreciate the way that Cernera appeals to the Eucharist for guidance in understanding the qualities of true leadership in Catholic education. He might have turned first to his own considerable experience as a university president, or to our best theoretical literature on management principles, or to the marks of virtue outlined in Aristotle's ethics. These other resources, and many more like them, will have their own truth to tell, and no doubt will inform the kind of leadership we seek. But it would be a mistake to give principles other than the basic beliefs of our own tradition a primacy in setting the course for our reflection on leadership and its enactment.

I know that some may find in these words a certain kind of post-liberal suspicion that tries to deal with the problem of religious particularity by circling the wagons of tradition against the world. I believe, though, that Catholic doctrine does not allow for such a view, as the Council's "Pastoral Constitution on the Church in the Modern World" (*Gaudium et Spes*) teaches so clearly. Assigning priority to the tradition, however, in our search for the truth of our lives is a matter of priorities. As we turn to our tradition first for guidance in our leadership responsibilities, we do not find only one resource and we do not find one simple answer. We find as much plurality as unity in the resources it offers and thus in the direction it gives: the life of Jesus in not one but four versions; not one but seven sacraments; saints who practiced holiness in surprisingly different ways; hundreds of pages of the sacred scriptural Word with several interpretive senses; and a sacred tradition that continues to develop anew with each passing day, as it will until the eschaton. As well, we find as much ambiguity as clarity in the resources our tradition offers, and thus, in the direction it gives to defining the task of leadership. This ambiguity can often be frustrating as we face concrete decisions, or plan for the future, or try to respond to someone who expects a precise definition, in twenty-five words or less, of what it means to be a Catholic institution of higher education today. But we work to eliminate that ambiguity at our peril, for a dimension of it is the divine mystery in which all creation courses and toward which all authentic leadership leads.

Notes

1. *Decree on the Apostolate of Lay People* [*Apostolicam Actuositatem*] (1965), in Austin Flannery, ed., *Vatican Council II: The Conciliar and Post Conciliar Documents* (Wilmington, DE: Scholarly Resources, 1975), 13.

2. *Dogmatic Constitution on the Church* [*Lumen Gentium*] (1964), in Flannery, ed., *Vatican Council II*, 32.

Response to Anthony J. Cernera

DIANA L. HAYES

I have learned from my own experience in the church that I come from a different perspective than many in this room, not because of my theological training or lack thereof, but simply because of my own cultural and historical context. I think we have our work cut out for us as we work to ensure that Catholic colleges and universities continue to do the work of educating leaders for the twenty-first century, both for the church and for the world.

The United States is unique among nations in that it has given rise to the development of a vast network of Catholic schools at every level of education. Catholic parochial and higher education systems in the United States have accomplished what may have seemed initially an impossible task: that of taking the children of immigrants and transforming them into politicians, lawyers, doctors and nurses, teachers and professors, businessmen and women, and of course, priests and religious. I think sometimes we do not know what we have wrought. The U.S. Church is no longer a ghetto church. It is now a meaningful part of the American mainstream and is serving as a critical moral voice in the public square, as well as a voice of reconciliation and healing.

The 1960s brought about dramatic changes in how we saw ourselves and lived as a Church. But it also brought significant changes in our country's social, political, and legal frameworks. As has been noted, the election of John F. Kennedy as the first, and to date, only Catholic president, marked a symbolic arrival of Catholics into the mainstream of American life. Also, Pope John XXIII's convening of the Second Vatican Council and charging it to reach out to the modern world and to work to help ameliorate its many problems, rather than to retreat from or condemn it, marked a critical shift in the Church's self-understanding. It is a shift, however, that is still seeking fulfillment. Many who supported and worked for this *aggiornamento* continue to fend off efforts of those who wish to return to a Church that was overly juridical and excessively clerical. Arguably there can be problems with change if it takes place too quickly, and/or with inadequate reflection. But there can also be problems with refusing to be open to the signs of the times, a denial of the ever-changing reality in which we and our Church reside.

A proverbial phrase attributed to Heraclitus says that it is impossible to step into the same river twice. The water has flowed beyond you and a new flow approaches. Like a river, today's Catholics have moved on. They have grown and matured, and the Church itself is a different place than it was forty or even twenty years ago. We cannot expect to develop Catholic lay leaders using models for training priests or religious, nor can we expect the laity to act, think, or behave as they did.

In their pastoral letter of a few years ago, *Our Hearts Were Burning*, U.S. bishops appeared to recognize the maturity of the Catholic faithful and called for programs of religious education at every level that would go from cradle to grave, rather than stopping abruptly, as had happened for too many after Confirmation. With such preparation, I think it would make the task of Catholic colleges and universities much easier, as there would be a much broader foundation upon which to build. Recent events in the Church, however, make me fear that the bishops are not exactly listening to their own teachings.

Other events took place in the 1960s that had an impact on all of us, Catholic or not. The major event, of course, that overlapped Vatican II in many ways, was the civil rights movement that involved Christians and Jews, believers and non-believers, blacks and whites and so many others. Martin Luther King, Jr., called for the emergence of God's beloved community in our midst, urging especially his fellow Christians to also live by the teachings of Jesus, which they fervently proclaimed but often profaned. King's argument was based, of course, on Genesis 1 and 2, the creation of all humanity by God, and probably unknowingly he echoed the Vatican fathers who asserted in the 1965 document, *Gaudium et*

Spes, that all are endowed with a rational soul and are created in God's image, all have the same nature and origin, and being redeemed by Christ, they enjoy the same divine calling and destiny. As such, there is a basic equality between all people and this conviction must be given even greater recognition.

This is at the heart of my response. The civil rights movement was a liberating catalyst that sparked liberation movements, not just for African Americans, but also for women, Latinos and Latinas, Asians and Native Americans. It provided a paradigm for how people could come together as a community rooted in faith and walking out with that faith in order to change the world around them. For Catholics who participated quite often against the will of Catholic hierarchical leaders, this movement and the Second Vatican Council revealed to them a Catholic Church with a very diverse face—a multi-hued, multi-cultural Church whose members came from every land and whose cultures and traditions helped to make up the tradition of the Church itself. Catholics of color were especially affected by these events and movements. No longer willing to be missionized and recognizing rightly that they had come of age in their Mother Church, they demanded the right to speak for themselves and to worship in a unique style and manner and harmony. Their songs, their dance, their ways of speaking about God and Jesus Christ moved beyond the rubrics of the Roman Catholic rite. In other words, they called for a true inculturation of the gospel into their traditions and heritages that had not been done heretofore.

It could be said that a stumbling giant had been awakened: not only the Catholic laity who saw and claimed their right as the People of God to participate in the mission of the Church, but also Catholic laity of color began to reclaim their history. It is important to remember that the Church was born from within Judaism as a world church and then went into a kind of European captivity before returning once again to becoming a world church. When one thinks about the ancestry, for example, of persons of African descent in the Catholic Church, we were there the first year with the Ethiopian eunuch who became a Christian.

The recognition of the essential role of the laity has profound significance for our self-understanding as Church. Anthony

Cernera is correct in noting that "99% of the Christian community who are baptized are responding to the call of the Lord and living their lives of discipleship in the world and in the Church." Equally important are those committed and active Christians who are persons of color seeking opportunities historically barred to them to serve their Church as lay persons at every level. Sadly, we have to acknowledge that the history of many of our leading colleges and universities prior to the 1960s is blighted by the sins of sexism and racism and their fallout. Women and persons of color were not admitted to many Catholic institutions of higher education until the 1960s. The result is a vacuum that will haunt us for decades. Where are the black, Hispanic, Asian, and Native American leaders—lay or religious? I know of only one black president of a Catholic university, and that is Norman Francis. His university, however, is one that is also historically black, Xavier University of New Orleans. Xavier somehow manages to produce the most black leaders in the health and science professions of any university in the United States. It would be beneficial, I would think, for all of us to learn how they accomplish this and to borrow some of their models.

It is critical that we recognize the need to encourage leaders in Catholic higher education from a pool that is inclusive and diverse. Strong demographic shifts toward Hispanics and African Americans are already upon us, both in the nation and in our Church. It has often been said that by the middle of the century the United States will have a majority of Hispanic-speaking people. The Catholic Church will reach that point decades sooner. Are we prepared or even preparing for these shifts? We are increasingly aware of them, but what exactly are we doing about them? How do we encourage blacks and Hispanics, Asians and Native Americans that there is a future for them in our colleges and universities—that they will be encouraged and supported, that they will be welcomed and relied upon?

It is of critical importance that the model programs needed are developed in ways inclusive of other styles of learning, other styles of teaching, other styles of working in community. It is imperative that we look for students to encourage, not just at the college level, but also the high school and perhaps even the elementary level, identifying, targeting, soliciting, promoting, assuring them that there is a future for them in this Church. We need them now and we will need them in even greater numbers in the future as faculty, administrators, trustees, and in time, hopefully, presidents of our Catholic colleges and universities. This means, however, changing how we recruit students and faculty, as well. I believe it also means that learning about other cultures than the European one can no longer be seen as a luxury or an elective, but as a necessity. And the learning must start at the top, in the president's office, and work itself all the way down to the faculty and administrative staff.

As you can see, I am rather passionate about this. I have reason to be. I am a convert to the Catholic Church, called in my thirty-first year from the life of a Methodist attorney to that of a Catholic theologian. I am not exaggerating when I say that it was a great shock to me as well as to my family. I think I am still reeling from it. For me, the Catholic Church was a total mystery and I had no idea what it was about, what I was being called into, or why I was being called into it. I did not know whether it was Satan or God at first. I believe it was God who brought me into this Church, perhaps to be a harasser of all. I do not know. But I was even more surprised when I arrived at Catholic University of America in 1980, only to discover that I was the first lay woman, as well as the first African American woman, to be in the pontifical degree program in theology. So I spent five years studying with about forty seminarians, to the consternation of them and many of my professors who accused me of being in classes I was not supposed to be in, such as the Sacrament of Reconciliation. I was even more shocked when I arrived at the Catholic University of Louvaine in Belgium, and found much the same thing. Once again, I was going to be a first.

All of my Catholic life—really most of my life—I have been a first in many areas, and it can be wearing. Being a convert is difficult and I struggle to understand this monolithic hierarchical institution, as do many. But it is also a human entity, and that is what saves it, I think. It can also be freeing, however, to be a convert. I have a great deal of knowledge of the pre-Vatican II Church but I have no memory, for which I think I am grateful.

Thus, I have never longed for what was, or even looked at what might have been. I have no desire to go back, because I was never there in the first place. The problem, I think, with many who want to go back is they weren't there either!

As a professor of theology at a Catholic university, I believe it is of critical importance for me to prepare our students for the challenges and realities of today. It is important to examine the problems and the good things about the past, but also to help them to look to the possibilities that lay ahead. I encourage them to learn from each other as Catholics, but also to learn about and become friends with Protestants, Jews, Hindus, Buddhists, Muslims, and all of the other students that are now filling the classrooms at Georgetown. I do not see this reality as a threat or as something that has gone wrong. I see it as a positive challenge to enable us to broaden our self-understanding, and theirs as well. We must prepare all of them for very different futures: One that is not color blind, but color filled, representative of the diversity that exists in God's self, as we are all God's creation.

Although I rejoice in the fact that an African American, Bishop Wilton Gregory, now heads the Conference of U.S. Bishops, I am also aware of the very long struggle that my people have undergone and continue to undergo along with other racial minorities, although the term minority is really an oxymoron now. I have been told by Catholics and Protestants alike that I must be a Protestant because I am African American, and how dare I say I am a Catholic because there are no black Catholics. In actuality, there are three million black Catholics. If we were to, for some strange reason, separate from this Church, we would be the second largest black Christian church in the United States, which stuns the Baptists immensely! There are black administrators at our colleges and universities—I have spoken at their annual conferences—but they are few in number. There are six black Catholic systematic theologians—which is probably why I am always so tired—four canon lawyers, and three Church historians. The list is pathetically short when one realizes that there are over three million of us in the Church.

All of us, however, are the Church. We are the People of God. As leaders of Catholic colleges and universities, all of us, regardless of gender or ethnicity, must lead the way for the rest of the Church. We have a mandate from God to make the Reign of God possible by preparing leaders to heal an increasingly broken and torn world in Church. We are preparing for the in-breaking of God's spirit among us.

PART III

Spirituality and Lay Leaders in Academe

Spirituality and Lay Leaders in Academe

LAWRENCE S. CUNNINGHAM

> Religion is not something to be relegated to a quiet corner or a few festive hours . . . it must be the root and basis of all life; not merely for a few chosen ones but for every true Christian. — Saint Edith Stein

My topic is spirituality as it is linked to the academic life in general and leadership in academic life in particular. As someone who, fifteen years ago, left a state school to teach in a Catholic university for the precise reason that it was a Catholic school, this topic is of more than theoretical interest to me. Furthermore, I have a professional interest in the area of Catholic spirituality and have been involved both formally and informally in thinking about the Catholic character of universities. One of the most challenging tasks of my recent academic life came a little over a decade ago when I was asked to serve on a small committee to develop a mission statement for the University of Notre Dame—a task which took up a considerable chunk of my time in a total process that took just over a year. Thus, the invitation to come to Sacred Heart University to speak to this distinguished conference affords me the opportunity to reflect back, from a number of angles, on this most timely subject. For that opportunity I am deeply grateful and I congratulate Anthony Cernera and Sacred Heart University for convoking us into a consultation on this critical issue.

The Nature of Spirituality

The word "spirituality" is protean in character. For many today, it carries with it a sense of some deeper life than the mere round of quotidian activities; its catchphrase is "I am spiritual but not religious," which typically means that one desires some significance to one's life that once was supplied by religion but today is not.[1] This is not the sense in which I will use the term spirituality.

By Christian spirituality, I mean a way of life shaped by the Spirit-filled following of Christ in community. Within the Catholic tradition, further, I understand that following to be shaped by the resources that have become part of the tradition itself—resources that flow, first from the receptive hearing of the Word of God and participation in the sacramental life of the church, enriched by the many practices that the tradition has remembered and proposed as among the many ways to help us follow the One Way who is Jesus Christ.[2]

It is clear that the Catholic tradition proposes many ways to be a follower of Christ. There are many ways to follow the One who is called The Way.[3] Some of these ways have developed, over the centuries, into schools of spiritualities (e.g., monastic, Franciscan, Dominican, Salesian, and Jesuit) each with its own pedagogy of prayer, its preferred texts from scripture, its own peculiar charism, and so on. These schools have also flowered into more formal pedagogies that have been associated, in time, with forms of higher education. Many lay people today have aligned themselves in one fashion or another with some of the practices from these traditional schools: we have learned the practice of *lectio* from the monastic tradition; the power of contemplative prayer from the Carmelites; the link between prayer and care for the poor from the Franciscans; the centrality of conversion and discernment from the Ignatian tradition, and so on. One could say that in the decades since the Second Vatican Council people in the church have reaped vast benefits both from the work of *re-sourcement* carried on by so many in their attempt to recover the treasures of the various strands of Christian spirituality and by new experiments in Christian living that have sprung up after the Council.

It is further clear that spirituality cannot be narrowed only to mean cultivating one's own spiritual garden of the soul. The whole thrust of Christian spirituality today is linked to the central concern of linking spirituality to social justice, engagement with the world, and a preferential option for the poor. Any authentic Catholic spirituality must take into account the directions set forth in the Second Vatican Council's pastoral constitution *Gaudium et Spes* and the energies derived from the orientation of that pastoral constitution's declarations.

As we consider this embarrassment of riches offered to us, it would be well to keep in mind some wise words written in the early modern period by Saint Francis de Sales in the opening pages of his classic *Introduction to the Devout Life*:

> Is the solitary life of a Carthusian suitable for a bishop? Should those who are married practice the poverty of a Capuchin? If workmen spent as much time in church as religious, if cloistered religious were exposed to the same pastoral calls as a bishop, such devotion would be ridiculous and cause intolerable disorder.[4]

He then goes on to conclude: "A devotion which conflicts with anyone's state of life is undoubtedly false." Francis de Sales was, in fact, one of the earliest spiritual writers who explicitly argued that the practice of Christian spirituality (what he called the "devout life"—and be aware that the word "devout" had a deep technical meaning in his writings) had to be consonant with one's place in life. That may be a truism today but it was not so in the early seventeenth century, when it was far more common to assume that every person would draw on forms of spiritual practice that derived mainly from the monastic tradition.

Spirituality and Academe

This brings us to the question I wish to consider in these brief reflections: What kind of spirituality is apposite for a person in this time and place who happens to find him- or herself in the world of academe? And, further, to enlarge the question a bit: What kind of spirituality is required to form those who are or will be called to assume leadership roles in higher education?

At a general level, I suppose one could answer briefly and let it go at that: Be a sacramentally involved Christian, which ramifies out in love for the other; be an exemplar of social justice; pray; and watch for the coming kingdom. In other words, be and do as any serious Catholic would be and do. To put it into the vernacular: be a "good" Catholic. However, I want to focus with greater particularity on the Catholic life in the world of the academy. This tighter optic does not grant me permission to offer concrete strategies of spiritual practices, nor would I presume to do so. Instead, I would like to articulate some meta-principles that will find their particular exercise depending on place and circumstance.

Pope John Paul II reminded us forcefully in his 1998 encyclical, *Fides et Ratio,* that all learning has as its intended end that Truth which became incarnate in Jesus the Christ.[5] Furthermore, the rise of the schools and of the universities were ministries of the Church that formed part of the Church's strategy to keep possession of and advance the gospel, which is the repository of truth. It was further argued by the pope that the ideal marriage of human learning and divine revelation is best understood under the character of wisdom. A Catholic university, if it is to be Catholic in more than a denominational sense, should be a place where one is shaped by, and attendant upon, wisdom. I further stipulate, drawing on a wonderful line from Saint Thomas Aquinas in the *Summa*, that to be truly wise is to possess a kind of participation in divine wisdom which is God.[6] In another place, Thomas distinguishes that wisdom which is given by God as a gift of the Holy Spirit and that acquired wisdom which comes from human study, which is an intellectual virtue.[7] Wisdom, then, is both a gift and the fruit of honest intellectual labor.

The goal of such an intellectual tradition understood as sapiential within the Catholic university has been set forth in an economical way by the Second Vatican Council:

> The hoped-for result is that the Christian mind may achieve, as it were, a public, persistent and universal presence in the whole enterprise of advancing higher culture, and that students of these institutions may become persons truly outstanding in learning, ready to shoulder society's heavier burdens and to witness the faith to the world.[8]

It seems to me clear that the intention of the Council is to understand the Catholic university where the life of wisdom is to be pursued and also as a ministry from which well-formed persons are sent forth to incarnate gospel values in the larger culture. I take this all to mean that the pursuit of the intellectual life—in this case, in the setting of the college or university—is the pursuit of wisdom, which is, strangely but wonderfully, a gift of the Holy Spirit and a fruit of study. It is the somewhat mysterious dance (*perichoresis*) of openness to grace and the hard work of thought that constitutes the vocation of an academic. To model that dynamic into the arena of action is to be an academic leader.

My use of the word *vocation* is deliberate. Doubtlessly there are folks working at Catholic colleges and universities who are there because it is a job that keeps them indoors and the beneficiaries of a steady paycheck and health benefits. Some become academic leaders because they have the skills to administer. What has always impressed me, however, is the cadre of people that one meets on various campuses who reflect an institutional loyalty that can best be explained as manifesting a deep faith that what the institution is and what it purports to be and do are of profound significance. At my own institution, I see such fidelity among professors, student affairs workers, administrators, athletic personnel, and folks who provide, often self-effacingly, all of the services that makes an institution function. Those folks seem to have a vocation rather than a career. They form the living heart of the university community.

My contention would be that to the degree that people in the world of academe can bring to the fore an articulated consciousness that they all contribute to the ideal of the university—the pursuit of wisdom—to that degree they have a grace-filled role in the Body of Christ who is the Wisdom of God (see 1 Corinthians 1:24). That consciousness can easily be veiled over if there is not a general consensus that such is the case. To the degree that a university underscores a caste system, privileges the bottom line over justice to its cooperators, or exhibits a behavior far from its rhetoric (no matter how pious), the sense of community is diminished or curdled into sourness. The sense of vocation hardly thrives in such an atmosphere.

The first requirement, then, of providing a matrix for the working out of the Christian vocation is the persistent need not to allow community to turn into organization. The nurturing of community is a dialectical one. It supposes a leadership that believes in community, fosters it at both the macro and micro levels, and has some well articulated conviction that community (in this case, Christian community) is not only possible but essential. At the other level, there is then the need for those who are members of the community to share in it, support its bonding, and further its vision.

It is, in fact, the case that in the very near future the Catholic community incarnated as a university will be increasingly in the hands of lay people. One need only look at the rosters of the many Jesuit, Holy Cross, Benedictine, Franciscan, and Vincentian colleges and universities in this country (to name only a representative sample) to realize that the presence of members of the founding orders is in a state of steady erosion. The fact that Georgetown University in the recent past named its first lay president is a harbinger of things to come. This demographic shift should not be seen as some kind of disaster but as part of the larger reality in the church today as we move from the modern Catholic world characterized by baroque spirituality into the more pluralist postmodern world of post-Vatican II reality.

This shift does bring with it an urgent question: Will the future (and present) lay leadership bring with it a spiritual formation analogous to that enjoyed by those who were so formed within the religious community to which they had belonged? The question is not about finding "good" Catholics for leadership roles but of finding dedicated persons who have the formation necessary to articulate and model the Catholic idea of education as an education in wisdom where faith and reason breathe as two lungs of a single body. What characteristics should such persons have?

Spirituality and the Catholic Intellectual Tradition

In the first place, they should be engaged with and committed to the Catholic intellectual tradition. The precise shape of that tradition is a matter of intense discussion in our own day made all the more intense by reactions to *Ex Corde Ecclesiae*. Indeed, whatever one may think of that document—and it does have its critics, both friendly and hostile—it is clear that its most important result was to have people think deeply about Catholic higher education's self-identity. It is beyond the scope of this paper to discuss the Catholic intellectual tradition, but at the very least one must say that it is (to borrow Alasdair McIntyre's phrase) a tradition of inquiry that, in its shorthand version, may be described as the ongoing attempt to triangulate human inquiry, human formation, and the ongoing handing down of divine revelation in creation and history. That tradition has deep roots in the monastic *schola*, the medieval *universitas*, the founding of the great learning centers of Europe, and its present instantiation as inheritors of those traditions in the contemporary world.[9] Obviously, this tradition is not merely an antiquarian memory closet but a living tradition that shapes and is shaped by the actual exigencies of the world in which we live. There arises, then, the twin obligations of preservation and renewal.

In order to get beyond mere lip service to the mission statement of a given school, one would expect leaders in Catholic education to go beyond assent to its propositions to some actual engagement with its presuppositions and its intentions. Or, to put it in John Henry Newman's categories: to embrace the Catholic intellectual tradition in the sense that is desirable is to affirm it both in a notional and a real fashion. This real engagement with the Catholic intellectual tradition is easier to stipulate than to accomplish. More and more of our faculty come with their graduate studies having been done in secular or non-Catholic settings. It is not to be assumed a priori that they have much more than a passing acquaintance with the Catholic tradition in any fashion similar to those who had been shaped by the old Jesuit *Ratio Studiorum* or something similar. This is not only true of professors generally but even those who have finished work in theology or philosophy outside of Catholic influence.

One consequence of this sea change is the need for Catholic schools to provide formation for willing scholars to develop their scholarly work in ways that put it in dialogue with the Catholic sapiential tradition. Such experiments in formation, understood as intellectual dialogue, are, in fact, under way at places like Boston College (the Jesuit Institute) and my own institution (summer seminars for faculty on the Catholic intellectual tradition). There may well be other experiments going on in this or in similar veins; if there are, such experiments deserve careful study.

In addition to formation in the Catholic intellectual tradition there is also the *desideratum* that there be some vehicles for deepening the spiritual life of those who are in academe. In this area there is no single suggestion that would cover the resources of an individual school. If, however, a school is serious about its Catholic character, then there should be some connection between Catholic faith and the curriculum. By highlighting such a connection, I do not mean that there ought to be some attention paid to philosophy and theology—that goes without saying—but something more: a link between the curriculum and the Catholic world view, which would mean, in the concrete, a demonstrated concern for social justice and a commitment to the option for the poor.

One way to frame this issue is by asking some pertinent questions: Are colleges only training for the job market? Are our particular courses any different from those on a secular campus when, in fact, they can be different? Do any significant number of our graduates go into the serving professions either under the aegis of the church or in some compatible arenas? Is there any link between the general shape of our curriculum and service to the needs of the world? Have we given more than lip service to the crying need for formation in ethics beyond the platitudes often dished up in the name of business or nursing or professional ethics? Is there any conscious resistance to the noxious fumes of some areas of postmodern thought where values are thought to be mere constructions from culture and truth claims exercises in ideological obscurantism? These and similar questions are asked not for the sake of being accusatory but as a bench mark to inquire if all the energy we put into the maintenance of Catholic schools actually derives from commitments to the sapiential tradition of Catholicism. Do they make a difference?

I say that the questions I raise are not accusatory, and they are not. In fact, any person in Catholic education who raises them and then attempts to provide a satisfactory answer to them has already combined a deep sense of Catholic spirituality with a deep respect for the Catholic intellectual tradition. God bless the business professor who helps students develop strategies to empower the poor to rise up from poverty and begin little businesses for the neighborhood. God bless the biologist who helps students study ways of eradicating malarial mosquitoes in sub-Saharan Africa. God bless the social scientists who steer students into NGOs for a life of service here and abroad. God bless those faculty members in the humanities who not only model the life of the mind but who inspire students to follow in their footsteps in becoming future professors of literature, philosophy, language, and the other humane disciplines. God bless those professors who insist that teaching the young is a noble way to spend a life.

Every one of those blessings I direct at professors whom I know and respect at my own university. I could name others but this talk must not become a litany of blessing. What must be said, however, is that every professor who shapes and sends forth a student with a vision of serving shaped by the Catholic intellectual tradition of learning and service grounded in the presence of the Spirit is a leader in the deepest sense of the term. Obviously, from out of those ranks will come energetic persons who may be called to the increasingly onerous life of academic administration.[10]

A Final Note

If there is one fundamental point that requires some clear stress, it is this: there must be no artificial separation between one's spirituality (or "spiritual life") and one's larger life and calling. The spiritual ideal cannot be separated from the intellectual ideal in the life of the college or university; they are of a piece. To teach, write about, and do research in one's chosen field is to be on the path of truth that ultimately leads us to God. The whole cloth of the intellectual and spiritual life is a given in the Catholic tradition; it is best summed up by the title of a classic work in the Catholic intellectual tradition: Dom Jean LeClercq's *The Love of Learning and the Desire for God*.[11] That holistic vision of cultivating the life of the Spirit and the life of the mind has been iterated and modeled in figures as diverse as John Henry Newman and Saint Edith Stein, both of whom are held up as models in *Fides et Ratio.*

This fundamental datum of the Catholic tradition that grace builds on nature and, as Saint Thomas Aquinas says in a stunning affirmation, that every true thing uttered by anyone comes from the Holy Spirit—"Omne verum a quocumque dicatur a Spirito Sancto est"—is the bedrock not only of the intellectual life but the Spirit-filled life of every believer.[12] If we live with those kinds of convictions, not only are we living an authentic spirituality but we provide models for those others who have been entrusted to our care. So then let us make our own the prayer that Saint Augustine once uttered as he finished his great complex work on the Holy Trinity: "I have sought Thee—I desire to see in my understanding what I have held by faith."[13] It is in that desiring, oriented to understanding what is already held by faith, that every true pilgrim discovers the deepest meaning of spirituality.

Notes

1. I have explored this disjunction in "Stairway to Heaven," *Notre Dame Magazine* 31, no. 3 (2002): 25-29.

2. I have elaborated the notion of spirituality as a way of life in Lawrence Cunningham and Keith Egan, *Christian Spirituality: Themes from the Tradition* (New York: Paulist Press, 1996), 5-28.

3. The concept of the Christian life as a way of life has been brilliantly developed by Gustavo Gutierrez. See *We Drink From Our Own Wells* (Maryknoll, NY: Orbis, 1983).

4. Francis de Sales, *Introduction to the Devout Life* (London: Burnes and Oates, 1956), 14.

5. See the essays in *The Two Wings of Catholic Thought: Essays on* Fides et ratio, ed. David Foster and Joseph Koterski (Washington: Catholic University of America Press, 2003).

6. Aquinas, *Summa Theologica*, II-II q.23 2 ad 1.

7. Aquinas, *Summa Theologica*, I q.1 6 ad 3.

8. From the *Declaration on Education* [*Gravissimum Educationis*] #10. Note the balance between serving the world and witnessing the faith.

9. From the vast literature on this subject, I have been helped especially by John Langan, ed., *Catholic Universities in Church and Society*

(Washington: Georgetown University Press, 1993); Theodore Hesburgh, ed., *The Challenge and Promise of a Catholic University* (Notre Dame: University of Notre Dame Press, 1994); James Heft, ed., *Faith and the Intellectual Life: Marianist Award Lectures* (Notre Dame: University of Notre Dame Press, 1996); Patrick Carey and Earl Muller, ed., *Theological Education in the Catholic Tradition* (New York: Crossroad, 1997); and Anthony Cernera and Oliver J. Morgan, ed., *Examining the Catholic Intellectual Tradition* (Fairfield, CT: Sacred Heart University Press, 2000).

10. The alleged disconnect between academics and administrators has been vigorously challenged by Stanley Fish in his essay "The Intellectual Role of Administrators," *The Chronicle Review* (April 4, 2003), B-20.

11. Jean LeClercq, *The Love of Learning and the Desire for God* (New York: Fordham University Press, 1961).

12. Aquinas, *Summa Theologica*, I-IIae 109 1 ad 1.

13. Augustine, *De Trinitate*, XV.28.51.

Response to Lawrence S. Cunningham

Zeni Fox

In reflecting on Dr. Cunningham's valuable paper, there were two points that particularly resonated with aspects of my own experience. The first is that leadership at Catholic colleges and universities will be increasingly in the hands of lay people. Of course, here at Sacred Heart that has been true for its forty-year history. The second is that a sense of vocation is of great import. I will expand on each of these.

First, some perspective on the increasing role of laity, and decreasing number of priests and sisters, in order to place the experience in higher education in a larger church context. In June of 2000, the United States Conference of Catholic Bishops discussed the issue of the impact of fewer priests on pastoral ministry. The study document provided for them gives very telling statistics. Between 1950 and 2000, the Catholic population in the United States more than doubled, increasing by 107%. During the same period, the number of priests increased by only 6%. Furthermore, the average age of diocesan priests was 57, of vowed religious priests, 63. There were 433 priests over the age of 90, and 298 under the age of 30.[1] In some dioceses bishops are withdrawing priests from virtually all roles other than parish ministry.

As we all know, the number of sisters has declined greatly, from a peak of 181,421 in 1965, to 122,653 in 1980, to 81,161 in 2000.[2] Furthermore, in 1966, two-thirds of sisters were involved in educational ministries, by 1982 the percentage was 29%, and in 2000 only 11%.[3]

By contrast to these statistics, the number of lay leaders is increasing rapidly. As you know, there are lay presidents at the majority of Catholic colleges and universities. This statistic can be set in the larger context of lay leadership in ministry in the church today. The most recent study of lay ecclesial ministers (the title the bishops are using for professionally prepared lay persons in leadership roles in parishes) indicates that in 1997 there were 30,000 working in parishes, an increase of 30% in five years. In 1997, 27,015 priests served in parish ministry, a decrease of 12% in the same five-year period, and a number smaller than that of lay ecclesial ministers.[4] Since 1997, the number of lay ecclesial ministers has continued to grow. In addition, great numbers of lay people head diocesan offices, work on diocesan staffs, serve as campus, hospital, and prison ministers, and lead various Catholic institutional ministries. Based on statistics regarding those entering vowed religious communities and seminaries in recent years, there can be no question but that this trend will continue in the foreseeable future.

The second point made by Dr. Cunningham that I wish to reflect upon is the importance of a sense of vocation. I agree with his use of this concept relative to the work that people do, rather than only one's state of life (married, single, priest, or religious). I interpret this "sense of vocation" to mean that an individual has a belief that what he or she is doing is what God desires of them, that their gifts of nature and training and grace, call them to this particular work. I would add that, because those at a Catholic institution of higher education are serving in a Catholic institutional ministry, it is desirable that they see their work, their vocation, as part of the mission and ministry of the Church.

In my experience, my colleagues at Seton Hall University do not generally use the category of vocation relative to their work. A number of years ago, I had a conversation with a dean who spoke with passion and conviction about the needs in his field, which he was striving to meet with creative initiatives. I observed, "That is your vocation." He demurred, seemed a little embarrassed, and the conversation moved on. On another occasion, I had been asked to lead a retreat for faculty, and chose the topic, "The Vocation of the Teacher." These events do not draw many people; this one did not. Tellingly, a number of those who came said they had not thought of themselves as having a vocation. My work in a master's level program for Catholic school principals has given me the opportunity to explore this question of vocation, the vocation of the teacher, the vocation of the educational leader. With this group, too, most do not attest to a prior belief in their having a vocation. However, in the process of dialogue with these educators, I have found that they recognize, and claim, the vocation to which they have been responding. They *have* answered the call with the choices they made, with their service to others, with their commitment to truth, as educators. But they had not named this as a response to a vocation, as a calling. I see in this process of recognition something that Karl Rahner once described: they come to a conscious awareness of that which is already present by grace.

I have contrasted these experiences with my work with lay persons involved in various other aspects of the church's ministry, for example, hospital chaplains, pastoral associates, and directors of religious education. They speak a language of vocation. They say things like, "I think this is what God wants me to do" and "I do not know where pursuing this degree in pastoral ministry will lead me, but I think that this is what I am supposed to do." For a number of years, a subcommittee of bishops at the U.S. Conference of Catholic Bishops has been studying the issue of lay ecclesial ministers. They have been involved in several consultations, and sponsored varied events, in an effort to understand this new phenomenon of laity in pastoral leadership roles. Based on their listening, one conclusion they have drawn is that "Lay ecclesial ministry is experienced by many to be a call to ministry, a vocation."[5]

Does it make a difference? Are my university colleagues and the Catholic school principals doing a poorer job because they do not have the same consciousness of vocation as the lay ecclesial ministers do? I would say yes and no. Certainly, without a conscious awareness of vocation, committed and effective teaching, research, service, and leadership can be practiced. Individuals can work from a sense of Catholic identity, implicit or explicit, and strive to hand that on to others. But with awareness, with a sense that this it what I should be doing, a new level of meaning opens for us. Parker Palmer's *The Courage to Teach* is an extended meditation on the theme of vocation. He reminds us that when we teach from a deep place of faithfulness to our call, which is a faithfulness to who we are, then we are in communion with powers beyond ourselves, co-creating the world.[6]

For Palmer, this sense of vocation is deeply human, not necessarily related to a particular religious understanding. As Catholics we affirm that all persons are called into being by God, and therefore all are called into partnership with God in the stewardship of creation. All are called to use their gifts for the good of the community. This understanding of vocation could inform the work of all persons involved in Catholic higher understanding, making possible a community of commitment formed of those from varied, or no, religious tradition. But in addition, for committed Catholics who are part of educational communities, a sense of their vocation, individually and collectively, allows a focus on the work of the school as part of the mission of the Church, part of the Church's effort to continue the ministry begun by Jesus. In communion with powers beyond themselves, by grace, they become conscious partners in co-creating the kingdom Jesus proclaimed.

However, a question we need to ask is, Why is it that so many Catholic educators do not have a conscious awareness of their vocation to teach, and sometimes to lead? I think that this is also an issue that must be examined in the larger context of Church life. Most Catholics, when asked what a vocation is, would respond that it is a call of God to become a priest or a sister. Some might say that it is a call to vowed religious life, marriage, or the single life. The idea of a call to a particular *work* is not taught, or preached. When we "pray for vocations" as a community, almost always the prayer is for vocations to the priesthood and religious life. Our life as a church does not invite young adults into processes of discernment, into reflection on what is their call, except in regard to clerical or religious life. Our life as a church does not invite mature adults into processes of reflection on the meaning of the call they have followed in their work life, and a probing of how to live the call more fully and faithfully.

Institutions of higher education alone cannot change the mindsets of Catholics, but they can be a significant factor in fostering an awareness of vocation to a particular domain of work, as an important dimension of spirituality. The initiatives undertaken at many schools, designed in response to the call for proposals on this topic by the Lilly Endowment, illustrate various ways in which this can be done. The fostering of a sense of vocation among teachers and administrators is part of a larger whole; it embraces a fostering of a sense of vocation among students, and among all who share in the work of the institution. The stories of efforts to do this, as undertaken by various institutions, need to be shared with the larger Church community, so that bishops, priests, and all of the people will begin to think of vocation more holistically. This understanding relates to many themes emphasized in recent church documents. Notable examples include the call to renew the temporal order in the *Decree on the Apostolate of Lay People* of Vatican II (see especially article 7), and the call to go out into the vineyard, which is the world, and restore creation to its original value, as proclaimed by Pope John Paul II in *Christifideles Laici* (see especially articles 2 and 14). Perhaps the so-called vocation crisis in the Church today will provide the impetus to explore the vocation of the laity more fully, at every level of Church life.

There is a further specification of the sense of vocation that I think is necessary. Catholic colleges and universities have been called Catholic institutional ministries; that title recognizes that these efforts are part of the mission of the church. As we all know, there has been much dialogue in recent years about what this means; some of the discussion has focused in a particular way on what it means in light of increasing lay leadership. Over ten years ago, Cardinal Joseph Bernardin envisioned "seminars and similar academic programs to help new lay leaders of Catholic schools, hospitals, and social service agencies to understand in greater depth the basic components of Catholic culture, identity, and mission."[7] Such efforts have begun, it is true, but I think that the meaning of mission, especially mission relative to institutions of Catholic higher education, needs ongoing exploration by *all* members of these institutions. What is the vocation of each individual serving the institution? What is the relationship of the institution itself to the mission and ministry of the Church? There is not a formula for defining response to these issues, but rather an answer that each institution needs to discern, corporately, and then to embody.

I would like to conclude with a story that I think describes an institution that had done this. Some years ago I served as a member of an accreditation team at a seminary. The self-study was thorough, and had included reflection by representatives of all those who comprised the community: support staff and students, faculty and grounds keepers, administrators and food service personnel, board members and diocesan leadership. Customarily, the accreditation team holds its final meeting with the rector and anyone he chooses to have present to hear a summary of the evaluation. When the team arrived for this meeting, over fifty people were present, including some in the uniforms of their work, some faculty we had interviewed, and some graduates who had taken part in the process. All waited to hear the comments about *their* school, the mission *they shared in*.

Vocation and mission do not belong to a few, but to many. And, in classic Catholic practice, vocation is discerned communally, not simply appropriated individually. The task involved is, therefore, both personal and communal. A spirituality rooted in a sense of vocation and of sharing in mission is properly Catholic, focused on the individual, in community. This needs to be fostered and nourished in and by our institutions of higher education, and by the larger Church.

Notes

1. *The Study of the Impact of Fewer Priests on the Pastoral Ministry*, unpublished document prepared by eight committees of the Conference for the general meeting of June 15-17, 2000, pp. 4, 17, 19, 27.

2. Patricia Byrne, "In the Parish but Not of It: Sisters," in *Transforming Parish Ministry: The Changing Roles of Catholic Clergy, Laity, and Women Religious*, ed. Jay P. Dolan, R. Scott Appleby, Patricia Byrne, and Debra Campbell (New York: Crossroad, 1989), 113; *The Official Catholic Directory* (New Providence, NJ: P.J. Kenedy and Sons, 2000), 2093.

3. Byrne, "In the Parish but Not of It," 113; *The Official Catholic Directory*, 2093.

4. Philip J. Murnion and David DeLambo, *Parishes and Parish Ministers* (New York: National Pastoral Life Center, 1999), iii.

5. *Lay Ecclesial Ministry: the State of the Questions.* A Report of the Subcommittee on Lay Ministry (Washington: United States Catholic Conference, 1999).

6. Parker Palmer, *The Courage to Teach* (San Francisco: Jossey-Bass Publishers, 1998), 183.

7. Charles J. Fahey and Mary Ann Lewis, eds., *The Future of Catholic Institutional Ministries* (New York: Fordham University Press, 1992), 24.

Response to Lawrence S. Cunningham

MONIKA K. HELLWIG

I heard four themes in Dr. Cunningham's presentation. The first was a definition of spirituality with which I find myself cheerfully in agreement: Christian spirituality is discipleship of Jesus; in the power and grace of the Holy Spirit; within the community, that is shaped by scripture, tradition, and sacrament. Such spirituality reaches out in compassionate friendship to the needy, along with all those concerned with transforming the world in the light of the coming Reign of God.

A second theme I heard had to do with vocation of the laity and the ways that the academic life, the intellectual life, may be seen as a lay vocation. Dr. Zeni Fox has addressed that, so I will not. A third theme had to do with academic life as a quest for truth, and more particularly that truth which is wisdom. Such a search is not only for personal, spiritual, and intellectual growth and becoming, but also for engagement in the culture and for concern with public affairs. That is something that I will return to. The fourth theme that I heard consisted of interesting practical reflections about where we are in our project with Catholic colleges and universities in the present context and where we may want to be in the future. Though I will not address this here, it could be a topic for fruitful conversation in the future.

I return to the third theme to flesh out how the academic life of our Catholic higher education institutions is or can be an exercise of Christian spirituality. The essence of Christian spirituality, the essence of living the Christian life, is faith, hope and charity. Faith, hope, and charity are about an individual and communal vision and longing and commitment. What we really mean by faith goes far beyond believing that certain propositional statements are true and immediately relevant to ourselves. That is part of the understanding of faith, but much less than the whole. In its essence, faith is openness to the continuing self-revelation of the Divine—always and everywhere, in all things, when convenient and when inconvenient, when intensely private and intimate and when directly concerned with public affairs. We are concerned, therefore, with opening our eyes progressively wider to the self-revelation of God in everything.

The physicist's work, for instance, reaching into the immensity of creation and also into the most intimate composition of matter, is, properly understood, a contemplative study that looks and wonders and tries to understand, as a prelude to collaboration in the work of divine creation. Such study tries to understand the wisdom of the creator and to locate human life within the immensity of the whole and in relation to the teasing illusiveness of the inner composition of matter. It suggests respect for all that is, reverence about tinkering with the immense potential power revealed. It also asks for responsible screening of possible manipulations of nature in terms of their predictable and unpredictable impact on the quality of human life and the harmony of the whole.

Something similar can be said of the study of biology. The proper way to go about unlocking the secrets of life, the miracle of growth, and the mystery of ecological interdependence is with great awe and with great reverence for life as divine gift in all its manifestations. That reverence for life becomes so much the greater as the living things that we study are more a reflection of the Divine in sensation, consciousness, self-direction, choice, and so on. The reverence for life of the biologist is especially called for in terms of the impact of applications on human life and the ecological balance of forces that sustain human life. Everything that we do in our laboratories has consequences, often evaluated very differently from a commercial and from a Christian perspective.

One might say something similar for the mathematician who tries to grasp the patterns of relationship, the very possibility of number, the illusive and wonderful structures of space and time, the realities of proportion and relationship and relativity. The proper way to study those things and teach about them, drawing young people and the not-so-young into the subject matter, is not with the primary motive of mastering, but with the primary motive of seeing, admiring, and understanding to the best that we can, and accepting responsibility for the practical consequences that come from insight, discovery, projection, calculation, and application.

One might ask: Is that real academic work? Is that an appropriate motivation for what really goes on in the research and the teaching of a university? Can one engage in this way in the academic enterprise as it is in fact being conducted in the higher education world, and be accepted well enough to function there? I think so. The most serious perennial problem that we have in the academy is the desperate competition. There is the competition to be the first to publish something. There is the terrible hunger we have for recognition for our individual achievements, that intense desire we have to do it better than other people, to be popular as teachers and acknowledged as scholars. Those things get in the way of real scholarship, solid research, and truly good teaching. True progress and success in science, not only in the natural but also in the human and social sciences, depends heavily on collaboration, and collaboration depends on a certain level of selflessness and generosity. The work often needs to be interdisciplinary, and many of the most worthwhile projects need to be unhurried. This requires a larger and stronger motivation than does work for quick results and personal advancement.

Faith is the openness to God's continuing self-revelation in the creation as well as in our own consciousness and our conscience about right and wrong. In the works of nature and in the unfolding of history, it is precisely if we can accomplish that kind of detachment from personal promotion that is facilitated by the attitude of contemplation, reverence, and awe, that we will be able to do meaningful and good work in scholarship and in teaching. And faith, of course, points beyond itself to hope, the second of the key elements of Christian spirituality.

What do we mean by hope? Some of our traditional definitions seem remote from the real spiritual life of most Christians. But one of the more helpful insights developed in traditional spiritual theology is the following. Hope consists of a great desire and a confident expectation that together generate the energy to pursue the desired goal. Traditional spiritual theology also asks what that goal is, or what the content of Christian hope is, and answers that it is quite simply God, or union with God. Jesus, in the Gospels, makes it more practical and more contextualized when he directs hope to the coming Reign of God, to be realized in creation and specifically in the human situation, in human society and in human history.

How does this relate to the academic project? In the study of history, sociology, languages, literature, or even human psychology, we are looking at the potential for the realization of the Reign of God in creation. That is not the introductory explanation one finds in undergraduate sociology or psychology textbooks. But it is the much deeper reality of what we are doing. We are trying to understand, to observe more carefully, to make comparisons, and sometimes to do experiments. In all of this we are trying to know and analyze the problems and to understand the potential in the human situation from a stance of great and abiding hope.

Unfortunately, as we know, the contemporary academy is not the exercise of hope that it should be. It is commonly an exercise of dull acceptance of the status quo, as though our economic, political, and military systems were the inevitable traps in which we are going to live forever. Christians can do better than that because we see the world in terms of sin, and redemption. We are called to see our history, our economy, our international relations, our political affairs, in that way. By seeing the world in terms of creation, sin, and redemption, we have the basic requirements for an energetic public hope. The doctrine of original sin means that what one sees in the world is not the everlasting and inevitable entrapment into wars, poverty, racism, and oppression. It is quite the opposite. What one sees with Christian eyes is a challenge to discern what is of God's good creating, what is a distortion of human efforts to collaborate with God, and what is already of the redemption.

The challenge is to understand this and to find ways to act on that understanding. When we study history and the social sciences, we are not seeing a flat given, an inevitable, unalterable state of affairs. In fact, we can readily trace and document why and how the rich get richer and the poor poorer, the dominant countries and factions get more powerful, and the powerless and oppressed even weaker. Influential "think tanks" continue to purvey "trickle-down" theories, flattering those in power in the world, even while the facts daily contradict the claim. Christian scholarship and analysis must be done in the light of the truth, both the truth of the factual data and the truth of faith and hope. There is no contradiction between the two kinds of truth. There is a special vocation for those whose scholarly work is in the social sciences, because the social sciences are intimately linked to the process of redemption in the world. We see a challenge through them to discern what is both desirable and possible in human society. God's reign in human affairs and in creation is not an empty desire. The desire that is cultivated in us is coupled with a confident expectation that it can be realized, that there can be a transformation of society, that all things can be brought to meet the Reign of God, though not necessarily on any timetable we set.

As faith leads to hope, so hope must lead to charity. But what is charity? What is love? It is not primarily about words, but in commensurate deeds to the demands, the needs, the situation of our times. We speak of faith, hope, and charity, but the meaning may be clearer if we speak of vision, longing, and commitment. Nowhere do these central Christian virtues become more evidently necessary than in the academic enterprise, because the scholarship and teaching and the productive work in which we are engaged are not games that we play in the academy to have fun. To be sure, they are generally a lot of fun—more fun than most people in the world are ever able to have—but we cannot let it corrupt us into the seeking of fun for its own sake without responsibility. Even less can we let it degenerate into the seeking of status, recognition, of being there first, and so forth. No, the point of our scholarship, the point of our teaching, is what we can do for others. Certainly, as Professor Cunningham has said, the point of all of this is what we can do to grow spiritually and intellectually ourselves and how we can foster spiritual and intellectual growth in our students. But it is not for us alone as privileged people, but rather for service to the world. It is for cultivating a vision out of which can come a prophetic presence in our relationships to creation, to one another, and to our responsibilities in the world.

To repeat, faith is a matter of acquiring vision, of constantly deepening and clarifying vision, that is, the vision of God's self-revelation in creation, in the community, in ourselves, in history. Such faith leads to longing, to hope, to a forward thrust. And that forward thrust leads to commitment. As one lives out the commitment, it increases and further clarifies the vision, which in turn, leads again to a greater longing, hope, and thrust forward. Professor Cunningham earlier used the term *perichoresis*, the round dance, the dancing in and around and coming back to the same place, which is never really the same place again. We have more usually used that term when expressing the Christian's groping attempt to understand the mystery of God analogously in triune terms. But this same image of the round-dance is also applicable to our lives of faith, hope, and charity, and to our experience in any work, especially in academic work.

So what about the poor administrator? I talked about the scholar as scholar and the teacher as teacher. This, however, is certainly not to belittle or ignore the work of the administrator. The work of the administrator is a godly work in the literal sense, a divine work. As the teacher fosters the becoming of the students, so the administrator fosters the vocational development of a community of teachers and students. The administrator fosters that kind of community that Professor Cunningham spoke of, which is living out of the resources of scripture and tradition and sacrament, which is the community of faith, hope, and charity expressed concretely, but which is also a community of outreach. The administrator has a very special vocation. The administrator, more than anyone in the higher education enterprise, must have a broad and deep understanding of the meaning and implications of Christian faith in the context of the contemporary world. The administrator must have this grasp in order to guide the whole institution in a scholarly and educational enterprise that is really in service of the redemption in individual lives and in the world.

In this conference a number of speakers have ended with a good and inspirational story. I am not going to end with a story, because I want to say, both to the original listeners at the conference and to the readers of the volume, that you and I are the story and it still has to be completed.

PART IV

Lay Leaders: Issues and Perspectives

Trustees and Leadership for Mission

CHARLES L. CURRIE

At a conference on lay leadership we could argue that there is no more important form of that leadership than the exercise of effective lay trusteeship for our Catholic colleges and universities. In actual fact, the success stories of these institutions over the past thirty-five years have been due in no small part to trustee leadership, and specifically to the leadership of lay trustees.

Recently, we have become more aware of the need for trustees to focus on their responsibility for the Catholic identity and sponsoring group's mission of the institution. Responding to this need is a workshop designed jointly by the Association of Catholic Colleges and Universities, the Association of Jesuit Colleges and Universities, and the Association of Governing Boards to assist trustees in the discharge of that responsibility.

Until the late 1960s, the typical Catholic church or university was essentially an extension of the sponsoring religious community and was owned, operated, and staffed mainly by members of the religious congregation, i.e., the nuns, brothers, and priests. There was normally one civil corporation, and most often board membership was confined to community or congregation members. Lay "boards" were advisory at best.

The Second Vatican Council's vision for lay leadership, the desire to "mainstream" our schools, increased pressures to develop more professional faculty and administrators, and a benevolent interpretation of canon law led most Catholic colleges and universities to "separately incorporate." The institution and the sponsoring group no longer shared one civil incorporation, but each sought distinctive incorporation. They structured or restructured statutes and by-laws, transferred ownership, developed various formal and informal agreements, and established different varieties of reserved powers for the sponsoring group. All the while, a new partnership between the laity and clergy/religious was emerging. This separation was accompanied by an explicit commitment to maintain the Catholic and sponsoring group identity of the institution. It would simply be pursued in a different way.

These developments were accompanied by no little tension, but the end result has been an extraordinary period of quantitative and qualitative growth for Catholic higher education. Some commentators, such as Father James Burtchaell, have claimed that Catholic identity has suffered in the midst of this progress; others, and I include myself among them, claim that Catholic (and sponsoring group) identity has become stronger because we are more intentionally involved in its development. In either case, we come to today when the declining number of the members of sponsoring groups has led to an even greater concern to foster the founding mission and the Catholic identity of Catholic colleges, and sponsoring groups are more concerned about exercising responsible stewardship toward institutions they founded.

The varying degrees of influence sought by founding congregations or dioceses come under the rubric of "sponsorship," a term that has developed over the last thirty years to describe different ways the congregation or diocese relates to the institution in mutual efforts to keep the founding charism or spirit alive. There is no one model for how this is done, but Catholic schools have pursued two broad governance options.

The single-tiered governance model has one board responsible for the institutional mission. In American civil law the board holds in trust the purposes for which the institution was founded, which includes the Catholic/sponsoring group component of that mission. The sponsoring group itself is especially concerned to promote the Catholic/sponsoring group component of the mission, because it serves as the interpreter of the sponsoring charism of the institution. To recognize the legitimate interests and concerns of the sponsoring group, statutes or by-laws sometimes prescribe that the board have a certain number of sponsoring group members, and there are often formal agreements freely entered into by the board and the sponsoring group. Some by-laws allow for a form of "bloc voting" that requires the prescribed number of sponsoring group members plus one for certain significant votes.

A number of Catholic schools have been moving to a two-tiered governance model to protect the Catholic and sponsoring mission. An "inner board," or "board members," or "the corporation" reserves certain powers to itself, and leaves all other responsibilities to a board of directors or trustees serving as the second or "operational board." This model is meant to protect the interests of the sponsoring group. Examples can be cited where this arrangement has worked well, but many where it has not. It runs the risk of rendering the second board less effective by discouraging board members from fully committing themselves when someone else is "pulling the strings." This would seem especially likely to happen if the institution were to move from single-tiered to two-tiered governance, because such a move could be interpreted as a vote of no-confidence in the single board in the discharge of its responsibility for mission. If indeed reserved powers are to be used, it would seem best to keep them to a minimum, and to work at keeping the second board as strong as possible. The use (or abuse) of such powers could emasculate the operating board of the college or university.

Whether single or two-tiered governance is in place, the relationship between the board and the sponsoring group (or congregation) cannot be totally defined by juridical rights and obligations. It is more effectively based on mutual trust sustained by ongoing communication and support. Alice Gallin, author, educator, and for twelve years the executive director of the Association of Catholic Colleges and Universities, has suggested that the relationship might better be called "partnership" than "sponsorship."

Regular contact in good times can help build a level of trust that can weather storms that may occur. Boards need to find ways to welcome members of the sponsoring group or congregation appropriately into important deliberations. Sponsoring groups and congregations need to know that their influence and inspiration can be more important than control. Control can be counter-productive to the fostering of the sponsoring charism. The object is to keep vibrant, not merely preserve the tradition, and for that to happen, the quality of relationships is very important.

The Trustee Orientation Project we have been developing has two purposes: 1) to emphasize the role of governing boards of Catholic colleges and universities in fostering the Catholic and sponsoring group mission of their schools; and 2) to help make trustees effective and comfortable in that role. A collection of essays has been prepared to orient trustees to their responsibility for institutional mission, and a pre-workshop assessment survey has been developed to determine the distinctive situation of each institution and board as a basis for designing a workshop to fit specific needs. Twenty distinguished present and former presidents and trustees have been trained as workshop facilitators. The workshop is dedicated to developing a plan of action and board priorities to deal with the mission and identity issues raised by the survey results.

Boards range from doing very little to engaging in very significant and effective activity in exercising their responsibility for mission. I have served on both kinds of boards, as well as on some that fall in between. The comfort and interest of individual board members also varies greatly. Some want to be deeply engaged in the church-relatedness of the institutions and others, either because of a lack of interest, or because of an exaggerated deference to church leaders, leave it to them to deal with the "church stuff."

In general, with the board, as with the institution itself, some prefer to have the responsibility focused on a committee and some prefer to have the responsibility diffused throughout the board. Both approaches can work, but there should be some accountability built into the structure, i.e., various ways to ask and test candidly whether or not the particular strategy is working. The committee model runs the risk of allowing other board members to neglect their own responsibility (not unlike the temptation of some "non-academic" or "non-financial" board members to neglect their responsibility to learn something about the academic and financial health of the institution). The full board model runs the risk of so diffusing the responsibility mission that nothing specific happens.

If the committee model is chosen, then the committee (variously called "Mission and Identity," "Mission Effectiveness," "Mission Integration," and so on) needs credibility in terms of membership, charge, and integration with the other tasks of the board. Membership should not be confined to the sponsoring group, although they should certainly be a strong part of the committee. The committee should reflect the composition of the board itself and not include only those board members who are most enthusiastic about the mission. If there is two-tiered governance, mission issues should not be restricted to the "upper" or "inner" board, but should include members of both boards, thus picking up some of the advantages of the Notre Dame model.

Not only is the membership of the board important, but so too is its charge. I have been on boards where such a committee, or its chair, confined its role with the full board to offering short vignettes on the founder and/or mission, but without effectively engaging other board members in substantive conversation. I have also been on boards where the mission committee not only effectively educated the board in digestible portions, but also worked hard to relate its work to the other concerns of the board and was ready to raise mission issues in the midst of the board discussions on other agenda items.

Which brings us to a third aspect of credibility of the board committee on mission: its integration with the other tasks of the board. In the ideal order, there is an easy flow of mission concerns within the other discussions of the board—financial, academic, student life, and so on. This is where administrators can be very helpful, namely, in showing how mission concerns should influence every dimension of the school's activity. I recall how on one board a member would constantly raise the issue of the ethical dimension of whatever decision or policy was being discussed. The mission committee should be finding ways to do something like this. Is it too much to ask to have a concern for the mission bottom line, to match board concern of the financial bottom line?

Many, if not most, boards will be familiar with church-relatedness issues only in a vague sort of way. Their good will has to be supported by solid orientation, continuing education, and the good example of more senior board members. Presidential leadership is essential in this regard. Richard Ingram, of the Association of Governing Boards of Universities and Colleges (AGB), has emphasized that trustees will rise only to the level of expectation of their leaders, i.e., the president and the chair. Board members need to see the president as a role model in establishing a hard link between mission and all else that boards do, rather than something that is soft and fuzzy to talk about at other times, but not when the board is doing business. Even, or better, especially in time of crisis, when making hard and difficult choices, the mission has to come up to the fore.

In recent years, it has become increasingly obvious that a critical mass of women and men committed to the church-related mission is essential if that mission is to survive with any degree of vitality. In other words, a sufficient number of effective people strategically placed and capable of influencing the institution is needed to keep its mission and identity alive and well. Forty years ago in Catholic colleges and universities that critical mass was assumed to be present in the lived witness of the sponsoring religious and/or clerics, although even then it was also present, if in smaller numbers, in the witness of generous and committed lay colleagues.

Today, such a critical mass can no longer be assumed, but must be recruited and developed. The effort begins with trustees, i.e., in searching for trustees with at least the capability of being committed to the school's church and sponsoring group identity. Trustee profiles cover a number of characteristics as the board seeks to become as strong and effective as possible, but the commitment to mission needs to be discussed early in the recruitment process, with the understanding that effective orientation can lead from an initial openness to a more informed commitment.

In their monograph, *Relationship Revisited*, Holtschneider and Morey chronicled the decline in Catholic colleges and universities in the numbers of religious and priests, and noted that 28% of respondents to their survey reported that within ten years virtually no founding religious would work on campus or serve on the board.[1] Within that scenario, they suggested three options for institutions facing such declining numbers: become secular; find ways to protect the founding charism; become more universally

Catholic. Our workshop for trustees is directed toward the second alternative, suggesting "ways to protect the founding charism," which of course includes the school's Catholic identity.

We know that the future will not be like the past, and many find excitement and challenge in that. Catholics speak of the twenty-first century as "the century of the laity." Members of religious congregations and the clergy are being challenged to support and trust the laity in their emerging role. They are challenged to be generative rather than reactionary in transitioning their legacy into new forms. Such a transition clearly involves risks, but trustees can lead a partnership that can not only survive but prosper in new and exciting forms.

Notes

1. Melanie M. Morey and Dennis H. Holtschneider, *Relationshcip Revisited: Changing Relationships Between U.S. Catholic Colleges and Universities and Founding Religious Congregations.* Washington: ACCU, September 2000 (21): 3-39.

Sponsorship and the Religious Congregation

KAREN M. KENNELLY

My experience derives mainly from the Sisters of St. Joseph of Carondelet, a large congregation with general government but a decentralized structure. Provinces and vice-provinces are directly responsible for the sponsorship of institutions through which the mission is carried out. Institutions include five colleges and universities in addition to some fifteen hospitals and long-term health care facilities.

The congregation's demographic profile affords reason for both optimism and caution regarding the future of sponsorship. Provinces currently average about 460 members each, a reassuring figure when it comes to exercising the responsibilities of sponsorship. On the other hand, our median age is high, ranging from seventy in the Albany and Los Angeles provinces, to seventy-two and seventy-six in St. Louis and St. Paul respectively. We continue to be encouraged by the small but growing number of women now entering the congregation, as well as by the rapid growth of lay associate programs begun in 1974. These now include 451 women and men, many of whom are active in our sponsored institutions.

My approach to sponsorship is also colored by my familiarity with the five institutions of higher education sponsored by our various provinces, each of which has moved toward lay leadership in different ways and with a different pace: The College of St. Catherine in Minneapolis-St. Paul; Fontbonne University in St. Louis; Avila University in Kansas City; The College of St. Rose in Albany, New York; and Mount St. Mary's College in Los Angeles. A sixth institution, St. Mary's Junior College in Minneapolis, became the Minneapolis campus of St. Catherine's in 1986.

The influence of Vatican II on sponsorship would be difficult to exaggerate. All would agree that the understanding and practice of sponsorship has been deeply affected by such Vatican II-endorsed concepts as the basic equality of all Christians by virtue of baptism and the need for subsidiarity and mutuality in decision-making processes and corporate structures.

Equally portentous for sponsorship was the Vatican II call to religious congregations to renew themselves in the light of their founding spirit or charism, the call of the gospel, and the needs of the times. The subsequent membership decline in U.S. congregations (about 50% during the last quarter-century) is partially attributable to the conciliar summons to renewal and has had significant repercussions for the extent, nature, and quality of sponsorship arrangements. A diminished zeal for institutional or corporate ministry among many religious, an indirect result of the response to the Vatican II call to renewal, undermined sponsorship in the smaller and more vulnerable congregations.

Remarkable shifts have occurred over a relatively short period of time. From the perspective of religious congregations, a shift from control to influence with respect to sponsored universities and a concomitant shift from implicit assumptions to explicit measures with respect to mission effectiveness occurred. From the perspective of the laity, shifts took place from closed to open presidential searches; from holding a minority of top administrative positions to holding a large majority of such positions; from constituting approximately half of the faculty to around nine-tenths; and from the expectation that they would grasp the mission of the sponsoring religious congregation by osmosis to the expectation that they would learn from formal programs on mission initiated by the religious congregation.

We are generally too close to these broad trends to interpret them with confidence, much less to identify all their long-term consequences. For this reason, I hope you will appreciate my desire to use the remainder of my essay to address behaviors conducive to healthy sponsorship. My comments are based on the insights I have gained as a member of the Carondelet congregation and a teacher and administrator in its sponsored institutions of higher education. My basic assumption is that new and strengthened forms of lay-religious collaboration have evolved since 1965 for the Sisters of St. Joseph of Carondelet, forms that have the potential for sustaining our Catholic mission in higher education long after those of us present here today will have retired from active ministry.

In the interests of time, I propose to focus not so much on the forms sponsorship now takes—there is, after all, an abundant literature on two-tiered boards, reserve powers, sponsorship agreements, and the like—as on the characteristics of successful lay-religious collaboration and how we can reinforce these characteristics. Resources included at the end of this paper are intended to supplement this brief presentation.

Marks of Successful Lay-Religious Collaboration

Based on personal experience on both sides of the desk—as a faculty member and academic dean in one of our sponsored institutions, and as a college president of another; as executive director of the Carondelet university association for several years; and as province director and now a member of our congregational-wide Leadership Team—I would suggest a half-dozen guiding ideas and several concrete actions for consideration by religious and laity seeking to promote Catholic identity in the spirit of founding and/or sponsoring congregations. The guiding ideas highlight the need to communicate, report, anticipate, subordinate, trust, and believe. The concrete actions I propose emphasize the need to celebrate, integrate, and formalize. Allow me to offer a few words of explanation about each of these.

Communicate: The analogy of "location" as the major factor in enhancing the value of real estate comes to mind. Asked to cite three factors adding to property value, the astute realtor named "location, location, location." Asked to name three behaviors or guiding ideas essential for good lay-religious collaboration, I would name "communication, communication, communication." Confidentiality is not usually a problem. Hidden agendas are. Communication goes both ways—there must be an element of mutuality here as in all of the other guiding ideas I discuss.

Report: By this I mean behavior that expresses the concept of reasonable accountability of religious congregation to institution and vice versa. An example that comes readily to mind is the annual report called for by the Los Angeles province while I was president of Mount St. Mary's College. Preparing responses to questions relating to mission; assembling and sharing materials such as audit reports, enrollment, and program data, and the strategic plan; and the ensuing personal dialogue between religious and institutional leadership teams afforded a priceless opportunity for mentoring and building mutual trust. The reporting site was traded from year to year, one year at the provincial headquarters and the next at the college campus, to give each other the "feel" of our respective environments.

Anticipate the inevitability of clashing goals and motivations. I'm sure we could all cite examples of situations when lack of foresight led to a serious breakdown of communication and even the severing of sponsorship relationships. Better to anticipate than to find yourself always reacting to crises. An obvious example is that of anticipating the likely need to modify by-laws when they restrict the presidency to religious and few or no suitable candidates appear to exist within the congregation. Discussing the pros and cons of an open search well in advance of presidential transition helps both the congregation and the board of trustees deal with a very sensitive issue in a constructive manner.

Subordinate the interests of any one individual or special interest group to the common good of the congregation and of the institution. Two examples that come readily to mind are the recent very generous donation of $20,000,000 to The College of St. Catherine by the St. Paul Province, and the amalgamation of St. Mary's Junior College with The College of St. Catherine in 1986. Both actions expressed in ways highly visible to the general public the confidence of a religious congregation in its sponsored institutions and the willingness to sacrifice in order to ensure a bright future for each institution. Both actions have been proven wise by the vigorous growth of St. Catherine's as a women's college proud of its Catholic heritage and its association with the Sisters of St. Joseph.

Trust that lay women and men are capable of "owning" or "carrying" the mission. Many examples illustrate and confirm the merits of such trust, beginning with the initiative taken by our

Los Angeles province during my presidency at Mount St. Mary's to reduce the proportion of sister-trustees from one-third to one-fourth, and to further revise by-laws to allow for a lay president. The result of both actions was to enhance lay trustees' sense of responsibility for Catholic identity and mission and to attract outstanding presidential candidates.

Perhaps it goes without saying, but we need to set lay leaders up for success rather than for failure at the same time as we express trust through by-laws revisions. Educational programs for trustees, administrators, and faculty, preceded and accompanied by open dialogue within the sponsoring religious congregation, are two fundamental ways to foster broad understanding of mission and personal responsibility for promoting fulfillment of that mission in every facet of university life.

Believe in the distinct missions of both the religious congregation and of the institution of higher education. There is no point in sponsoring an institution of higher education unless that college or university functions at a high degree of excellence with respect to academic as well religious facets of its mission.

With guiding ideas like these in place, lay and religious leadership can work together to:

Celebrate and honor the past, present, and desired future contributions of religious in the annual rituals, programs, and environment of the campus.

Integrate the congregation's particular charism or spirit into the fabric of the institution. An example I like to cite because of its relative uniqueness is the "Reflective Woman" course at The College of St. Catherine. Readings for the course typically begin with an essay by an alumna member of the province entitled "All Women Can Be: The Spirit of the Sisters of St. Joseph," and the first chapter of a college history, *More Than a Dream: Eighty-five Years at The College of St. Catherine.*

Formalize understandings and structures that will facilitate successful lay leadership and the continued exercise of positive influence by religious. Important examples in this regard are the "sponsorship agreements" that have been negotiated in the two Carondelet provinces that dropped reserve powers and the two-tiered board structure in the aftermath of Vatican II.

In conclusion, this is an exciting time and I look forward to our continuing dialogue, one that may be enriched by careful consideration of the following texts.

Recommended Reading

Mission and Identity: A Handbook for Trustees of Catholic Colleges and Universities, Association of Governing Boards of Universities and Colleges, Association of Catholic Colleges and Universities, and Association of Jesuit Colleges and Universities (Washington: ACCU, 2003). See especially chapters by David J. O'Brien, "A Catholic Academic Revolution," and Melanie Morey and Dennis H. Holtschneider, "The Meaning and Patterns of Catholic Sponsorship Today."

Bridget Puzon, ed., *Women Religious and the Intellectual Life: The North American Achievement* (New York: International Scholars Publications, 1996). See especially Karen M. Kennelly, "Women Religious, the Intellectual Life, and Anti-Intellectualism: History and Present Situation."

Tracy Schier and Cynthia Russett, eds., *Catholic Women's Colleges in America* (Baltimore: Johns Hopkins University Press, 2002). See especially chapters by Mary J. Oates, "Sisterhoods and Catholic Higher Education, 1890-1960"; Karen M. Kennelly, "Faculties and What They Taught"; and Melanie M. Morey, "The Way We Are: The Present Relationship of Religious Congregations to the Colleges They Founded."

Paula Kane, James Kenneally, and Karen M. Kennelly, eds., *Gender Identities and American Catholicism* (Maryknoll, NY: Orbis Books, 2001). See especially the section on "Education and Gendering."

Sisters of St. Joseph of Carondelet, St. Louis Province, *Sponsorship Handbook* (St. Louis: Motherhouse of the Sisters of St. Joseph of Carondelet, 2001). See especially chapters on "CSJ Ministry Through Sponsored Institutions," "Guide for Mission Integration Plan for Sponsored Institutions," and "Change in Sponsorship Status."

Sean Peters, "Sponsorship as an Evolution in Ministry" and "Some Models of Sponsorship" in the five-part series published in *Carondelet East* (Albany Province, January-May, 2003).

Tracy Meade, Helen Humeston, Shanan Wexler, and Cecilia Konchar Farr, eds., *The Reflective Woman*, seventh edition (New York: Copley Custom Publishing Group, 2000). Used as part of The College of St. Catherine's core curriculum, this edition includes Joan Mitchell, "All Women Can Be: The Spirit of the Sisters of St. Joseph," and Rosalie Ryan and John Christine Wolkerstorfer, "More Than a Dream" (the latter is an excerpt from the authors' history of the college).

Sponsorship in the Twenty-First Century

SHEILA MEGLEY

My interest in sponsorship is primarily, though not exclusively, focused on colleges and universities originally founded by women religious communities. Most of us are familiar with the general story. These colleges and universities were established toward the end of the nineteenth century and the first half of the twentieth century. The original purpose was to provide Catholic higher educational opportunities for Catholic women. By the end of this past century, these colleges followed one of four paths: they closed, became coeducational, merged with other institutions, or were one of a minority of remaining Catholic institutions for women. (Approximately 135 Catholic women colleges existed at the middle of the century, and about eighteen remain at this time.) This attrition is even more dramatic for the Catholic colleges and universities originally founded for male students. All have become coed. And, while I do not have an exact count, I would venture to guess that more women's colleges closed or merged than the men's colleges closed or merged.

There are Catholic colleges and universities that were not established by religious communities. Sacred Heart University is a concrete example. It was started when a bishop called together a group of lay people to establish and nurture higher education in the Catholic tradition. Catholic University of America is another unique situation, as it is a university founded by the United States Bishops. These institutions, however, are exceptions to the general pattern of the establishment of a Catholic college or university.

The general pattern of the establishment of Catholic Universities and Colleges in this country included a religious community as the motivating factor. The relationship of the higher educational institution and the sponsoring religious community is and was complex for several reasons: both institutions have different missions; distinct constituencies; distinct personalities, often reflected in the personalities of the leadership of each institution; and different perspectives on their historical interrelationships. Both institutions' leadership emerged from different populations and environmental mores, and claim an intellectual and spiritual Catholic heritage. However, religious communities viewed the establishment of a higher educational institution as the vehicle to live out the apostolic mission of their religious communities, while higher education institutions viewed their existence as a means of enabling others to discover and live out their Christian mission in the world. How each of these realties worked or did not work together defines the unique historical relationship for each individual institution, both for the religious community and the higher educational institution. It was about mid-twentieth century when Catholic institutions began to formalize their corporate structure and the relationship with the religious community. And it was only in the late 1960s and early 1970s that the word "sponsorship" came into popular use to describe this relationship.

Sponsorship became a word used to name the transition of religious community ownership and staffing of the institution to a formal relationship of influence sometimes expressed in redefined corporate structures or "sponsorship agreements." When our Catholic institutions began to form boards of trustees, some required that a specific number of the founding community be on the board as "members of the corporation," thus achieving influence and/or control on both tiers of a two-tier structure. Often it was also either written or assumed that the president of the institution would, or should be, a member of the founding religious community. It became clear by the 1970s that these institutions could no longer be staffed only by religious of the founding communities. The redefinition of the corporate structures or the sponsorship agreements was the direct result of the challenges facing the religious community, the higher educational institutions, and the world in which they both functioned.

Whatever the circumstances, the formation of the governing body was directly a result of the aspirations of the founding community and the development of the university or college. At this time, the establishment of a formal governance structure resulted from a variety of reasons. Some communities wanted to be protected from the liabilities that would be incurred by the educational institution. Some educational institutions recognized the need to develop a board that could assist in bringing outside financial support and expertise to the institutions. Some wanted to ensure that the influence of the religious community would continue. Others were trying to clarify who "owned" the university or the college. My point is that none of our Catholic colleges or universities and none of the religious communities are the same today as they thought they would be at the beginning of their endeavors, nor is the world in which they function. In fact, neither is the American Catholic Church nor even our understanding of what the Catholic faith means for each of us individually and for America collectively.

Perhaps it can be said that American Catholic higher education came of age in the twentieth century. As the Catholic colleges and universities, as well as the religious communities, came of age, their relationship was defined, either formally or informally, by their governance structure, which was either assumed or encased in corporate structures and by-laws. As we begin this twenty-first century, I believe that those Catholic institutions remaining under the sponsorship of religious communities (male or female) must resolve the ambiguity often associated with two-tiered boards (members of the corporation and board of trustees).

It is my conviction that by the end of the twentieth century, whatever governance structure had evolved, and however the interrelationships between the university and the community encased this governance structure, Catholic higher education and the religious community were reducing all of these concepts to the word "sponsorship." But "sponsorship" involves more than an organization providing money to an institution to advertise its logo and as a result gain public recognition and goodwill. In addition, the immediate direct influence of faculty and staff predominantly involves lay people. The paradigm has shifted.

Therefore, "sponsorship" by a religious community of a higher educational institution is not fitting terminology for Catholic higher education in the twenty-first century.

I believe each institution should first acknowledge that the relationship between the founding community and the higher educational institutions is now rooted in its governance structure or its sponsorship agreement. That relationship should be examined carefully with a view to understanding the similarities and the differences between a religious community and a higher education institution. Why do we have such an articulated or assumed relationship? Is it to protect the interest of the religious community, or to protect the interest of the higher educational institution? Does the existing relationship enable the institution to move forward? Is the relationship designed for control and influence by the religious community, thus adding another layer to decision making and, by default, disempowering and second-guessing those whose expertise we say we value?

What is important is that all the efforts and all the time, energy, and commitment over the years have formed a historical legacy. This legacy is the gift, a precious treasure, passed on in faith for others to continue. Rather than "sponsorship," perhaps we should talk in terms of "legacy" in the twenty-first century. The "legacy," the "gift" of the sponsoring community is its unique charism lived out in higher education, ever changing, ever growing, and passing through time from one generation to another, enriched by those who add to it today just as members of the religious community added to it in the past. When a gift is given, it is not to be taken back. We do not watch how a person uses it. We do not control or influence the gift once it has been entrusted to another. We give it in faith, praying and hoping that those to whom it has been entrusted will cherish it. To a certain extent, it is not as risky as it may first appear. These colleges stand in the Catholic tradition, one that embraces both the religious community and the higher educational institution.

I am currently on a Catholic high school board of trustees. The institution is sponsored by its founding community. Recently, the founding community has been insisting that the board design a plan to ensure the accountability to them of a plan focused on the spiritual development of the individuals of the board as well as the collective board. However, I am not certain that is the role of the religious community. Since the "members of the corporation" of the secondary institution are the same individuals as "the religious community leadership team," it is never clear who is speaking for whom. Further confusion arises when the method used to communicate this call for accountability to the board is inconsistent with the mutually agreed upon governance structure of the secondary institution. Rather, the board should design a plan to attract individuals to the board whose values are already compatible with the legacy or gift of the religious community and the educational mission of the institution. A board is responsible for development of the institution, consistent with its mission. But I am not certain that it should be accountable to an outside structure whose primary interests are not the primary interests of the board.

I am reminded of one of the parables of the gospel that I had always found hard to understand. It is the parable of the vineyard. The workers who came in the morning could not finish the job of picking all the fruit from the vines. So they brought in more workers to complete the task in the late afternoon. At the end of the day, all received the same credit or wage. I always thought that was unfair, until I realized one day that what mattered most was that the task was complete—the harvest was saved. And those who began the task could not finish it. Others have to complete the work. All talk of welcoming the involvement of the laity in the work of the gospel becomes clanging cymbals, when we act in a manner that second guesses, controls, or directs that laity to whom we have entrusted our institutions. It behooves us to remember that none of us built these institutions dedicated to our enduring concerns. I am reminded of an old adage that should guide us: "I am responsible for the house that I did not build, but in which I live." Our work is never finished. Nor is it "our" work. It is God's work. We need to trust others to carry it on when we are not present or "hovering."

Catholic higher education in the twenty-first century must have board members who recognize that they are entrusted with a historic philosophical gift—a legacy of the founding community—and that they have a responsibility to ensure that that gift is enhanced, promoted, and permeates the institution while they are in office. The task is yet to be completed in Catholic higher education, but there is not a shortage of workers. Others will continue. If it is from God, it will succeed. Just as there was a time when only religious envisioned the educational institutions as a means of living out their apostolate, so too must we realize that others also can view the work of education as a means of living out the gospel message.

It is true that the paradigm of the relationship of religious communities to higher educational institutions has changed. However, it is not true that everyone can, or wants to, recognize this change. Old paradigms are held tenaciously as perceived reality, usually by myths—things that were never true, but had an element of truth. For example, in this age of the laity, it is regrettable that some religious and some laity still believe and act upon the assumptions that:

- Religious are more spiritual than lay people.
- Lay people are not educated to the spiritual truth of the gospels.
- Clerics and religious are the only ones with the ability to articulate the gift—the legacy of a religious community.
- Lay people on boards of institutions founded by religious communities should defer to the religious on the board.
- Religious on the boards of trustees speak for all the religious and for the religious community.
- Catholic colleges and universities need clerics or consecrated religious in leadership position to be truly Catholic.

These misconceptions prevent the laity from finding and articulating the contemporary expression of the legacy: the gift of the religious community.

The Catholic college or university should be the place where the Church thinks, where all can find models of individuals living the gospel message, where faith is valued, where human kindness and compassion define the institutions, where all can be completing the work God has given us to do in our time. They should be places where all who are associated with the institution are able to live out their apostolate.

Catholic Through and Through

WILLIAM J. SNECK

A new challenge faces the 222 American Catholic colleges and universities. All but twelve of these were founded by a religious order or congregation, yet with the declining numbers of these clerical and religious members of the campus community, the institutions must find a way to preserve their individual identities as Catholic, a problem that didn't arise when many priests, nuns, and brothers walked the campuses. As the previous General of the Jesuits, Father Pedro Arrupe, used to ask, "How to do?"

The Maryland Province of the Society of Jesus is working toward an answer to this challenge. The specifics of the plan are presented here with the hope that a similar project might be instituted at other colleges and universities.

Our five colleges and five high schools are teaming up with one of our retreat centers, the Jesuit Center for Spiritual Growth at Wernersville, Pennsylvania, to offer two weekend "Conference Retreats," one in November and one in February, to members of boards of trustees, faculty and staff, alums, and parents of students on the topic of Ignatian Spirituality. A Conference Retreat offers points for reflection and guided suggestions for prayer. Time is also provided for groups within each institution to share the application of the conference points back home. The topics covered are: the life of Ignatius Loyola, the founder of the Jesuits, studied via a movie; Ignatian Spirituality; Ignatian Prayer; Individual and Communal Discernment; and the Consciousness Examen, an Ignatian method of practicing discernment in daily life.

One of my wise teachers once suggested that Catholic spirituality could be summed up in four brief and memorable axioms: love is possible; evil is reversible; forgiveness is available; and hope is real. Presented this way, Catholic spirituality is understandable and can be embraced by members of a Catholic institution who are not themselves Roman Catholic or even formally religious.

Under this broad umbrella of Catholic spirituality, each college or university's founding order then interprets its spirituality according to the dynamic vision of its earliest charismatic leaders by focusing on certain aspects of the gospel, and living them out through its members and its institution's spirit and way of proceeding. Thus, Franciscans are struck by the poverty of Jesus and try to embody his spirit in their lifestyle and behaviors, individual and communal. Benedictines embody the balance between contemplation and action, prayer and work, as their motto, *Ora et Labora,* indicates.

Ignatian Spirituality has been described, again by an insightful teacher of the author, as having the characteristics of a flair for prayer, a yearning for learning, and an attitude of gratitude. How do the sessions of the conference retreat spell out these particular characteristics of Ignatian spirituality? The Catholic tradition has always loved to present its ideals and values through their living exemplars, the saints. Thus we begin with the stirring and heroic life of Ignatius Loyola, his conversion from a soldier seeking fame and glory into a soldier of Christ aiming at his glory, *Ad majorem Dei gloriam*, "For the greater glory of God," a phrase that occurs countless times in his writings. We deliberately distinguish between "Jesuit spirituality," to be practiced by members of the order, and "Ignatian spirituality," its adaptation for our lay colleagues. This application is made easy because most of Ignatius's insights and principles were experienced and lived while he was still a layman.

The second conference on "Ignatian Spirituality" develops the three notions sketched out above by connecting them to the founding documents and the order's history. Thus a "flair for prayer" is rooted in Ignatius's *Spiritual Exercises*, the manual recording his prayer experiences in the cave at Manresa near the monastery of Montserrat, Spain, and guiding the retreats of countless Jesuits, their colleagues, and students. A "yearning for learning" hints at the order's dedication to education throughout its history, a suitable rallying point for the educators participating in the conference retreat. An "attitude of gratitude" reflects an optimistic perspective on the world, despite all its sin and mistakes, because followers of Ignatius "find God in all things," another favorite phrase of Ignatius, and praise God for his presence and providential activity.

Ignatian prayer has definable and teachable methods for beginners and advanced Catholics. Some of these will be shared with the participants, and they will be encouraged to practice them during their reflection period. Discernment is a method for begging God's guidance in discovering and living out his concrete will in the particular choices, large and small, facing an individual, community, or institution. One of Ignatius's interesting steps in any discernment process mandates that after gathering all relevant information, the discerner considers first the negative reasons against a proposed choice before listing the positives. This characteristic has the advantage of not letting the good features of a possible course of action sweep one's judgment away into optimistically embracing an alternative before consideration of all the reasons, positive and negative.

Finally, the examination of consciousness is not an examination of conscience that looks only for sins and faults. It is the practice of discernment in daily life with the intent of reviewing the various movements of spirit in one's heart during the day since the last "examen." Again, there are several steps: 1) a prayer for light in which one invokes the Holy Spirit for guidance in the exercise; 2) the outpouring of a grateful heart for God's gifts this day, large and small. This is especially important for putting into perspective a hard, stressful day; 3) review of the "intense" moments of the day. When did I feel particularly elated, angry, joyous, depressed, fearful, hopeful, enthusiastic, depressed, etc.? This is the heart of the examen and discernment. Since even the just person "falls seven times a day," there will be moments revealed when one has not been living up to one's Catholic Spirituality, one's highest ideals and values; 4) an expression of sorrow for sins, faults, failings discovered; and finally, 5) a resolve for tomorrow is formulated after a preview of the coming day's challenges and possibilities.

The examen can also be employed by a group, such as a board of trustees during a series of meetings, a faculty department, and so on. The goals of discernment and the examen are a habit of reflectivity, a clarification of and living out of one's institution's values and spirituality. Ignatian spirituality thus addresses multi-layered concerns: in our complex times, it promotes personal self-growth, an institution's unity and development, our communities' flourishing, and our world's move back from violence and toward peace and justice.

This concrete program is sketched out here in some detail to provide a paradigm for other schools to tap into the riches of their own founding traditions. The conference retreat format could be used, while the specific content would vary, of course, depending on the spirituality of the founding order. An experience could be crafted with the help of retreat house, parish, or campus ministry resources. Of course, what is learned in only a weekend would have to include extensive, committed, and conscious commitment to follow-up when one returns home.

Our plan at the Jesuit Center is to provide a similar weekend next year for first-timers, with a second "advanced" weekend (for participants from the first conference retreat) in order to address problems encountered after the first year of implementing the insights and graces shared by the participants. It is hoped that an approach like this would be useful for other colleges and universities eager to pass on the specific character of their institution to the next generation of students. These students will, in turn, take their place as lay leaders.

Cultivating Catholic Identity on Campus

KEVIN E. MACKIN

The subject of this short paper challenges us to say something profound about integrating our Catholic identity into the life of our academic communities. Sometimes in our desire to be profound, we miss the obvious. For example, in an early draft of *The Hound of the Baskervilles*, Arthur Conan Doyle had Sherlock Holmes and Dr. Watson camping out underneath a tent. In the middle of the night, Holmes woke up, shook Watson, and said: "Watson, look. What do you see?"

Watson replied, "I see millions and millions of stars."

"And what does that tell you, Watson?"

Dr. Watson paused, and then calculated. "Astronomically, there are millions of galaxies and countless planets. Horologically, it's three in the morning. Theologically, the universe is charged with the grandeur of God. And meteorologically it'll be a nice day tomorrow."

Holmes was silent. Eventually Watson asked, "Well Holmes, what does all this tell you?"

Holmes simply snapped, "Watson, you idiot, it tells me someone has stolen our tent."

Yes, sometimes in our desire to be profound, we miss the obvious. I would like to focus on some obvious practices and invite you to share yours with others. I presume that the overarching theme of the conference, "Lay Leaders in Catholic Higher Education," points to a discussion of ways in which Catholic identity can be preserved and strengthened, or, better still, more deeply celebrated.

I am putting aside for now a focus on public policy issues that affect higher education, e.g., a worldwide economic downturn, students who may be academically under-prepared and heavily dependent on financial aid, rapidly increasing tuition rates, and so forth. The Association of Governing Boards of Universities and Colleges (AGB) has summarized these issues effectively.

A Catholic college has to be a place where, whatever one's religious tradition, faith in a personal and provident God is not peripheral to the educational quest, but is taken seriously as an intelligent, morally responsible, and decisive option. Our colleges and universities must be places where people are educated in the practice of moral virtues that make one not merely an accomplished person, but a good person. As such, our schools must exemplify a Catholic identity that is rooted in gospel values.

We are aware of the changing relationships between U.S. Catholic colleges and universities and their founding religious congregations, which Melanie Morey and Dennis Holtschneider have researched. They found that 85% of Catholic higher education institutions attribute their relationship to ecclesial authority through founding, sponsoring bodies. The decline in membership of founding communities is challenging many of these colleges and universities to re-think their relationships in a way that will at least preserve their particular spirituality and Catholic character. In all likelihood, many of these colleges will become more universally Catholic and less congregational, and lay Catholics may well be arbiters of how congregational and Catholic identity survives.

I think that if Catholic colleges and universities are to preserve and strengthen their religious identity, mission, and culture, lay leaders have to be catalysts in developing strategies to ensure that this does happen. I would like to propose a few key strategies to promote such a goal.

Governance

- Review board by-laws to ensure that they include a statement about the Catholic identity of the college and the inclusion of some qualified members of a founding congregation on the board. The president at a Catholic college or university should be a practicing Catholic.

- Institutionalize an "Academy for Trustee Education." This would assure a resource of competent congregational and lay trustees who are dedicated to promoting the Catholic identity of the institution. The Association of Governing Boards of Universities and Colleges, Association of Catholic Colleges and Universities, and Association of Jesuit Colleges and Universities have published a handbook for Catholic college and university trustees titled *Mission and Identity*. The ACCU and AJCU, in particular, sponsor a workshop on "Mission and Identity."

Academics and Mission Efforts

- Form an endowed center for congregational-Catholic studies to act as a catalyst for strengthening the institution's identity. A center for Catholic studies could include three major emphases:

  An *Academic Program* that sponsors and encourages faculty and students to explore issues of faith and values in the context of congregational-Catholic traditions, e.g., Franciscan-Catholic or Jesuit-Catholic tradition, and so on. Interdisciplinary courses would focus on Catholic themes. These might encompass a range from biology and economics to law and politics. There might be joint appointments (for example, a professor of business ethics and religious studies). Also, faculty forums can explore the institution's spirituality concerning globalization and other contemporary issues. And I would encourage faculty to participate in Collegium. Grants, course reductions, and other types of support, can encourage research that explores the relationship between academic disciplines and Catholic social teaching regarding for example, medical ethics issues and religious themes in literature.

Spiritual and Liturgical Programs designed to reinforce the congregational-Catholic tradition. Liturgies and chorales, orientations, feasts and special days, retreats, and Rite of Christian Initiation for Adults programs should nourish our students, faculty, staff, and alumni/ae, "through and through." A well-staffed Campus Ministry program is important in highlighting and nurturing religious identity.

A *Service Component* that puts the message of the gospels into action. Faculty, staff, students, and alumni/ae should be encouraged to do informed volunteer service in the community. For example, at Siena College we have a Franciscan Center for Service and Advocacy, sponsored by the founding congregation and others.

- Provide a founding congregation web page, to promote Catholic academic and spiritual growth and articulate the values and tradition of the congregation. This site would be able to promote the history of the founding of the Catholic institution, and its progress.

- Establish a Catholic medal/award offered at the Commencement Awards Ceremony, celebrating prominent men/women who have contributed to the Catholic tradition on campus through their example, academic achievement, and social responsibility.

Student Affairs

- Strengthen the role of the Chaplain's Office for Campus Ministry, to facilitate clear understanding and support of Catholic moral values and the ethos of the founding charism. Professional staff living in the residence halls are key role models for students, so it is very important that staff reflect the mission of the college. Siena's Student

Affairs staff, working with the College Chaplain, are embarking on a Franciscan Values and Living campaign. An essay by the chaplain provides vision and values as a topic for staff meetings and interviews with Resident Director candidates. The staff focus programming and discussions on these values. The Chaplain's office also brings liturgies into residence hall space. This opportunity for students to become familiar with worship where they live has been very successful at Siena. A 10 P.M. Sunday Mass in one of our Residence Halls is standing room only.

- Craft a written agreement among students that articulates the rights of residents in a Catholic community. Founding congregations have much to offer regarding community life. Siena has Friars-in-Residence living with students, working together with staff. This can be an opportunity for students to learn that they can see God revealed in daily life with their fellow residents. We are called to facilitate this revelation of the deep importance of each person.

- Form a private "academy" led by dedicated Catholic faculty as a study group for capable student residents. This academy would prepare gifted students in practical Catholicism on campus in areas of spirituality, peace, justice, communication, and living together in society.

Sites/Sights of Catholic Education

- When people see our campuses, what Catholic sign value is offered? Is there a visible chapel, a grotto, other obvious indicators that we have entered a college with a Catholic identity? The University of Notre Dame has a grotto and a "touchdown Jesus." A cross on a dome or a statue of a saint is important because it reminds us and indicates to visitors that we cherish our traditions. Why not have a significant monument related to the founding group in an academic quad or other important space, to emphasize the nature of the institution? At Siena College, with a Franciscan tradition, we display reproductions of a crucifix that St. Francis of Assisi was inspired by. In our Student Union atrium, there are quotations on the wall by St. Francis, St. Clare, and St. Bonaventure. Each image and quote on our campus is a pathway for contemplation and learning. And yes, our physical plants present yet another opportunity to signify our identity and to enter into dialogue about our Catholic intellectual tradition.

Integrated Marketing

- Integrity is an important part of the Middle States Association accreditation process many are familiar with. We should be clear and consistent in expressing who we are as a Catholic college or university. To know who we are as an institution, to say truthfully who we are in marketing and recruiting and communications and other literature, and to follow through on who we are in day to day operations, is simply a matter of integrity.

Pre-enrollment

- Students should know clearly from their first point of contact with the college its congregational and Catholic identity. What distinguishes our institutions from state or secular private institutions? This should be obvious through literature, the college web site, visits to campus, and so on.

Orientation

- Our welcoming programs should include an introduction to the particular tradition of the institution (we can not assume that newcomers know what is obvious to us). For example, St. Francis and St. Clare are essential to understanding the Franciscan heritage. Their lives should be explicitly held up and connected to the learning and living throughout campus life.

Employment

- How do applicants understand our operating principles? How do we look for "a good fit?" We may look for related experience, and ask how he or she will support the mission of the institution. This presupposes a statement that is clear about being Catholic, Franciscan-Catholic, and so on. Hiring for mission is standard at all sorts of companies and institutions, because it is essential. People who work at an institution must advance the mission of that institution. How do our professionals articulate our Catholic principles and values? In what ways do we sponsor and encourage them to explore issues of faith and values in the context of our institution's congregational-Catholic traditions? The obvious answer is: education.

Academic Freedom and Speakers, Programs, Events at a Catholic College or University

- A Catholic college or university is devoted to principles of academic inquiry and the freedom to explore issues and matters essential to education and development of the life of the college. Such freedom cannot be unfettered, nor can it escape the very practical need for those responsible for governance of the college to place limits on events and activities that may, for example, threaten the fundamental principle of balanced and open academic inquiry; pose a threat to safety; may be grossly offensive or uncivil; may be inappropriate by ordinary standards of time, place, or manner; or may seriously undermine the mission of the college and thereby cause misrepresentation. Of course, while the right to place limits exists, such a right is also not unfettered, and should be exercised only in rare instances when no alternative exists other than to disallow a particular event. The overarching example would be common sense civility: an institution would not present something that mocks its own deeply held tradition.

Students and parents, faculty, staff, and alumni/ae, and the general public should rightly expect a Catholic college or university to be a place of solid academic study and celebration of Catholic principles and values. I began with a story about focusing on the obvious. So, I invite lay leaders of Catholic colleges to articulate the obvious and feel free to challenge, clarify, and improve the Catholic identity on their campuses.

The Mission of The College of New Rochelle

JOAN E. BAILEY

The College of New Rochelle (CNR) is most accurately described as mission-driven. The mission of the college from its founding until today has been to create an engaged academic community that provides access to an excellent liberal arts education, especially to those who do not have ready access to higher education regardless of who they may be. This has created an academic community of enormous diversity. Allow me to explain.

The Ursulines founded the college in 1904 as the first Catholic college for women in New York State. A rigorous liberal arts education was at that time available only to Catholic men or to women in secular institutions or institutions founded in other religious traditions, such as Barnard, Radcliffe, Mount Holyoke, or Smith. The population of young Catholic women was not yet being served by existing higher education, and so Mother Irene Gill founded CNR. The historical roots of the Ursulines trace back to sixteenth-century Italy and were grounded in the Ursuline charism of service to those who were not being served well by contemporary society, regardless of who they were or how society viewed them. Thus it was the charism of the Ursulines to address the educational needs of young Catholic women in the early days of the twentieth century, two decades before women could vote in the United States. Mother Gill believed that these young women would be best educated in the Catholic intellectual tradition of the liberal arts, preparing them as women of achievement and leadership in their families, their church, and their society. The first five decades of the college validated her vision, drawing young women from various ethnic groups but who mostly shared a Catholic school and church upbringing. The college flourished and welcomed young women from different cultural, ethnic, and religious traditions, following its mission and the Ursuline heritage.

In the late 1960s, the college added a graduate school, which by law had to be co-educational, and built on its traditional academic strengths of undergraduate psychology, art, and teacher preparation. As it did so, the inclusion of men and the attractiveness of program strength and reputation brought more students whose backgrounds and experiences differed from that of the traditional age (18-22) young women who attended what was now called the School of Arts and Sciences. At the same time, it became increasingly obvious that young women of color in the communities neighboring the college were not enjoying equal access to higher education. Many of these women were not graduating from high school with the credentials that would readily allow them to go to college. Thus CNR and other local Catholic colleges reached out to the local public high schools to admit a dozen young women who would enjoy the benefits of a CNR education and return to their community to become women of achievement and leaders for the future of the community. Based on recommendations and interviews to provide alternative predictors of college success, these young women were judged to be able to succeed in the demanding curriculum, if they were given both the opportunity and the necessary extra support. From this beginning at CNR and other local Catholic colleges, the New York State Higher Education Opportunity Program (HEOP) was born. This program is now in place statewide and has spawned numerous additional pre-college and college-based support programs across the country.

It is important to note here some of the important elements of this successful effort to promote access to college for students from "difficult" backgrounds. First, there was commitment of the institution from top to bottom to the mission of access and inclusivity, tied to the belief that the college is better for the presence of new populations.

Second, there was an emphasis on respecting individuals within the community by listening to them, responding to the needs of the newly welcomed groups of students—needs not only academic but also cultural, social and spiritual. This habit of listening and responding was as much located in the areas of the college that faculty and tradition may have seen as adjacent to education, but which the Ursuline tradition had always included in the very notion of education: education of the whole person. Indeed, it was observed that the academic areas moved more slowly to respond to the needs of these young women than did the areas of student support, such as residence life, student activity, and campus ministry.

Third, what helped to make this invitation successful was undoubtedly that these students were part of a group, a critical mass so to speak, albeit only about 10% of the entering class. Additionally, the college was moving simultaneously to reach other "new" populations who would help to provide visible support to this group of students in the School of Arts and Sciences. This project continues today, drawing into the community each year about twenty students whose educational background would not otherwise permit their inclusion.

From that intentional and very structured beginning, an increasing number of young women of color who have enjoyed much stronger educational preparation and who are regularly admissible see the college as welcoming to them and join us in great numbers. Although the School of Arts and Sciences is women only, mainly young women, there is great diversity of background in geography, economy, religion, race, and ethnicity.

But the story of CNR's diverse community is much more than this. In the late 1960s, another group of students began to appear on the campus in small numbers: older women who were returning to college to complete degrees begun before other obligations took them away. Often these women had left college to marry and raise families, or to go to work supporting parents or siblings, often brothers who were deemed as having a greater need for higher education. Following the mission and model of Ursuline education, which attends to each student and strives for the full development of the talents of each person, a faculty member in Arts and Sciences proposed a model of liberal arts education that would better serve the older adult students who brought maturity and experience as well as significant demands to the educational environment. This model of liberal arts education was built on the adult student as an equal partner in the educational process and saw the student as a "new resource" for the college community and for society. Thus was born the School of New Resources. This model recognized the abilities as well as the challenges facing an adult who would seek a college education, and this model was built on the mission of the college: commitment to the importance of the liberal arts as essential foundation for a real career. Liberal arts was to be understood, as it had always been at CNR, as preparation for a career, for life.

As this model was discussed and refined, plans were made to reach out to adults in the area around New Rochelle. The mood of the time as well as the law dictated that the program would be co-educational, although the students who inspired it were women. As plans progressed and word spread, the Municipal Employees Union of the City of New York (Local DC37) expressed serious interest. They had been offering a highly successful high school equivalency program for a number of years and sought a way to offer baccalaureate level liberal arts education to their members as preparation for further professional post-graduate preparation and career growth.

In the fall of 1972, both on the main campus and for the first time in the United States at a union headquarters, the full baccalaureate liberal arts program of the School of New Resources began with several hundred students enrolled and many more on waiting lists. Today the college proudly includes 4,500 adult baccalaureate students studying for an interdisciplinary liberal arts degree at branch campuses in Brooklyn and Manhattan, both at Local DC37 headquarters and at the Rosa Parks campus located in the Studio Museum of Harlem on 125th Street, in the Bronx at Co-op City, at the John Cardinal O'Connor campus in the South Bronx, and on the main campus of the college in New Rochelle.

What I have characterized as "adult centered" needs a bit of further explaining if one is to understand the enormous success of reaching out and drawing in new populations to create a highly diverse community. The essential ingredient has been commitment to the mission of the college, to provide a liberal arts education to those who are not being well served by existing institutions, and to treat each student with respect, i.e. to attend to the student as a whole person and to commit to the full development of that student to achieve her or his potential. In the case of the adult student, the effort has been to be a partner, to offer courses influenced, indeed shaped, by the learning needs and goals of the student by creating processes that assist the student in discovering and articulating those learning needs, and to provide a learning environment designed to support student learning. This has meant taking the learning environment to where the student works or lives: to the community.

For the traditional college-age women, it has often been efficacious for her to live with others near her own age away from the daily demands of family and society. For the older student, it has been efficacious to remove the obstacles of travel and schedule by providing a learning environment easily accessible within the community in time and space which adapts to the adult life rhythm. In both cases, serving very different students has meant creating very different models of education. Who the student is and what the student brings and needs are significant considerations in the educational design. This combination determines how well the student and community will meld. Thus, today the College of New Rochelle offers a traditional undergraduate residential living-learning model of education which also includes some commuter students and also offers an undergraduate inner-city learning model. This model, offered at different locations, offers the same curriculum (interdisciplinary liberal arts), but each location has a distinct climate and atmosphere, shaped to suit the students who study there.

The School of Nursing began on the main campus in 1975 and is co-educational and seeks to expand the male presence in nursing. It serves a traditional age population coming directly from high school or an associate's degree program, a large population of licensed Registered Nurses, and nurses who seek master's and post-master's education in nursing. It does this primarily on the main campus but also offers education in partnership with healthcare agencies and hospitals on their locations.

The Graduate School has continued to add appropriate programs in human service, education, art, and communications, and offers education courses in partnership with teacher's centers throughout the New York metropolitan area. In each school the college maintains its identity by following closely its mission while growing and changing. In each school the faculty and curriculum are adapted to the special learning needs of students, but always in the context of the college's mission. Students, faculty, and staff are diverse in every sense: different ages (only 10% of the students are between the ages of 18-22 and there are also students well into their 80s who attend), and various linguistic and geographic origins. The different cultures include several racial and ethnic groups.

Religious believers and those who practice no religion are welcomed into the community. Our president, Stephen Sweeny, is often heard to say that what holds the community together and gives us our identity is our mutual commitment to our mission, which is grounded in the Ursuline heritage. We are a woman's college, which we understand to mean that while we are not all women, we nevertheless take women's education seriously and honor the contributions and perspectives of women. We are committed to the importance of the liberal arts as foundational to education and career and as integrated into career preparation. We are Catholic, which allows us to engage in the dialogue of faith with reason and to examine beliefs and values in a spirit of ecumenism.

Finally, and not in order of importance, since all of these elements of our mission are commingled, we are committed to building a community out of diversity which honors the diversity and values the contribution of these differences to the whole. Institutionally we are committed to respect one another and respect for those qualities that define each as a unique individual. The institution unapologetically celebrates its catholicity while inviting all to the conversation about faith and reason, cultural heritage, the needs of society, and the ways education has as its aim service to others. We are not always successful but we are committed to continue the project. To the extent we have been successful—and our composition suggests we have certainly made progress—it is because our mission and our Ursuline heritage prod us to continue forward in hope.

Expanding Notions of Catholic Identity

SALLY M. FURAY

This conference focuses on lay leadership in Catholic higher education, a title that highlights the ongoing personnel changes in the operation of Catholic colleges and universities. It is my view, however, that Catholic identity is influenced by many other factors than the shift from religious to lay leadership in these institutions.

The last four decades have evidenced an accelerating shift in the moral consensus that characterized the beliefs and values of much of this nation for a good part of its history. The "captive audience," mostly Catholics, which Catholic higher education experienced for the first two-thirds of the twentieth century, has been replaced by pluralism and broader choices. Diane Eck's recent publication has demonstrated how this "Christian country" of ours has become the world's most religiously diverse nation.[1] Individual, institutional, and even religious value systems are deeply conflicted, creating new vulnerabilities and requiring revised approaches in virtually all aspects of institutional operations. Catholic colleges and universities are challenged to tread warily and self-consciously across three cultures with differing and often divergent intellectual and moral values: Catholic culture, American culture, and the culture of higher education.

The concept of culture is dominant in *Ex Corde Ecclesiae,* which underscores the reality that the relationship between faith and culture has become pervasive in Church thought in the last several decades. I will cite one passage wherein the document challenges the research agendas of Catholic universities. I believe this challenge should be applied beyond research and equally to issues which can and should be raised in our classrooms by competent professors and discussed by thoughtful students. The Catholic university, the document notes, is challenged to be

> immersed in human society; as an extension of its service to the church and always within its proper competence, it is called on to become an ever more effective instrument of cultural progress for individuals as well as for society. Included among its research activities, therefore, will be a study of serious contemporary problems in areas such as the dignity of human life, the promotion of justice for all, the quality of personal and family life, the protection of nature, the search for peace and political stability, a more just sharing in the world's resources, and a new economic and political order that will better serve the human community at a national and international level. University research will seek to discover the roots and causes of the serious problems of our time, paying special attention to their ethical and religious dimensions.[2]

As Catholic higher education endeavors to relate to conflicting and sometimes incompatible cultures, I like to remind myself of the broader view, namely, that institutions of Catholic higher education represent only one component of a wide and constantly evolving history of Catholic sponsorship of an extensive variety of humanistic enterprises. These include schools, hospitals, retreat centers, shelters, camps, barrio organizing projects, homes for the elderly, institutes and "think tanks," social service agencies, radio stations and other endeavors—all of which have been profoundly affected in the United States and other parts of the world by the shift in moral consensus, each enterprise in its own context.

For Catholic educators the result has been constant exploration of the meaning of Catholic identity in particular institutional settings, a virtual hallmark of Catholic higher education in the past three decades. John Langan suggests that:

> The concern over Catholic identity shows up in many different areas: the content of theology and philosophy

> courses, the behavior tolerated or forbidden in residence halls, the interpretation and fulfillment of the academic and religious commitment to social justice and community service, the choice of candidates for honorary degrees, the sorts of speakers who appear on campus [as well as the] relationships with church authorities . . . and the priorities the faculty brings to the task of choosing and hiring its own members.[3]

Such issues arise daily in the life of Catholic institutions, creating ambiguities and/or tensions that stem from the uncertainty, disagreement, and confusion among Catholic constituents inside and outside the institutions about the meaning of Catholic culture and about the contemporary role of the Catholic college or university. Sister Ann Ida Gannon, one of my heroines in Catholic high education, noted fifteen years ago that even when we view our constituencies in the light of the Second Vatican Council's emphasis on the People of God, we find differing and controversial expectations:

> A People . . . united . . . by a hope for the same end . . . may differ in culture, outlook, ability to change. They will be radical, liberal, progressive, moderate, conservative, ultra-conservative and each will want to be heard. Often they will use the same words but with different meanings; they long for dialogue but are upset when differing views emerge and are loyally defended; they espouse community but sometimes are really seeking uniformity. A People will never be tidy, neat, submissive but if it is truly a People the differences will not divide but will enrich the whole.[4]

Notes

1. Diane L. Eck, *A New Religious America: How a "Christian Country" Has Become the World's Most Religiously Diverse Nation* (New York: HarperCollins, 2001).

2. John Paul II, *Ex Corde Ecclesiae* [*The Apostolic Constitution on Catholic Universities*], September 25, 1990; rpt. in *Origins* 20, no. 17 (October 4, 1990), 265-76.

3. John Langan, "Reforging Catholic Identity: How Will Non-Catholic Faculty Fit In?," *Commonweal*, April 21, 2000, 4.

4. Anna Ida Gannon, "Some Aspects of Catholic Higher Education Since Vatican II," *Current Issues in Catholic Higher Education* 8, no. 1 (Summer 1987): 24.

Shaping Leaders for the Future: Native American Students at Creighton

TAMI BUFFALOHEAD-MCGILL AND RAYMOND A. BUCKO

Creighton University is a coeducational Jesuit university founded in 1878. In the past the university and Jesuits working on the local reservations encouraged students to attend Creighton. Since 1996 the University has made a concerted effort to recruit and graduate significant numbers of Native American students, nurturing them to become leaders at the university and in their communities. Creighton is located in eastern Nebraska at the gateway to the Upper Great Plains, home to many Native American tribes. The Jesuits and Creighton have a long-standing commitment to educating and serving Native American communities. These efforts have been successful and much can be learned from these processes as efforts are made to construct a model to form lay leaders in Catholic higher education.

The Jesuits began their long relationship with Native peoples in the early 1600s and in the 1880s extended their relationship to the Lakota People of South Dakota. They established schools on the Rosebud and then Pine Ridge reservations at the request of the Lakota people in the 1880s. Today Jesuits continue their work of education in collaboration with Native people both on reservations and at Creighton University. The Jesuit values, commitment to service, respect for religious and cultural diversity, and dedication to educating the whole person are consonant with the Native American sense of community, extended family, and respect for the holistic nature of the universe. Thus we have encouraged Native students to find a home at Creighton so that they may return to their reservations or urban areas to be leaders in their communities and among the larger Native American population.

Defining Success

To determine Creighton's achievement with Native students, we drew from Vincent Tinto's persistence predictors, which include academic performance and social integration.[1] Therefore, we looked specifically at academic performance, leadership development, and reported perception of the quality of their overall experiences as reported in the 1999-2000 climate survey.

For the purpose of this article, it is important to profile the typical Native American Creighton student. As of August 26, 2003, the enrolled Native American undergraduates (sophomore and above) at Creighton University are 63% female and 47% male. Sixty-seven percent are from reservations and 96% are enrolled members of federally recognized tribes. The largest tribe represented is the Lakota, with 42% of the undergraduate population. The mean cumulative grade point average for all Native undergraduates is 2.782, and the average number of credit hours completed is 61. The highest cumulative grade point average is 3.724 and the lowest is 2.000. The largest percentage of our students come from three states: South Dakota (46%), New Mexico (13%), and Wyoming (13%). Of our undergraduate students, 63% are Catholic.

For the 2003 graduating Native American undergraduate class, the average cumulative grade point average is 3.328, with the highest cumulative grade point average of 3.802 and the lowest 2.895. Of our May 2003 graduates, 25% are from a reservation and 75% are enrolled as part of a federally recognized tribe.

The 2003 freshman class is half female and half male. A more concerted effort was placed on recruiting from Nebraska, which had a definite impact. The states most represented for our freshmen are Nebraska (50%), South Dakota (25%), and Colorado (17%). The tribes most represented for our enrolled members of a federally recognized tribe come from the Lakota (33%), Winnebago Tribe (25%), and Omaha Tribe (16%). The mean high school cumulative grade point average is 3.628, with the highest cumulative grade point average of 4.00 and the lowest 3.12. The average ACT is 22; 58% of these students are from reservations; and 83% are enrolled members of a federally recognized tribe.

Recruitment

Native American youth frequently live in poverty, and are surrounded by unemployment, alcoholism, despair, and violence. Many Native American youth live in areas with limited educational opportunities. Exposure to long term economic and social distress contributes to an environment wherein Native American youth develop very low expectations for their future. Thus not only do they consider themselves incapable of being leaders but many do not even envision themselves attempting higher education, let alone succeeding.

Approximately 46.2% of Native Americans in Nebraska are living in poverty, which is higher than the rate for every other ethnic group in Nebraska.[2] "Native American youth," as Jodi Rave Lee wrote, "are caught up in a suicidal epidemic that is claiming more lives than any other ethnic group."[3] According to 1985-96 numbers from the Centers for Disease Control and Prevention, Indian Health Services reported that youth in Nebraska, North Dakota, South Dakota, and Iowa commit suicide at a rate six times the national average. Native youth throughout the nation and between the ages of 15-24 have the highest risk of suicide.[4]

Native American youth are also less likely to complete high school than members of other cultures. About 50% do not complete high school.[5] The attrition rate is 90% in some areas of the nation, which is higher than any other population in the United States. According to the 1990 census, 65.6% of all Native Americans 25 years old and above earned a high school diploma or higher, while 9.4% earned a bachelor's degree or higher.[6]

In 1996, Creighton was asked by John Blackhawk, the chairman of the Winnebago Tribe, and Fred LeRoy, the chairman of the Ponca Tribe, to consider how we could encourage college enrollment of their tribal members. In response to the community's request, Creighton University created the Native American Retreat, a program designed to encourage Native American high school students to prepare for higher education and consider college as a viable option.

The Retreat is a collaborative effort among Creighton University's Office of Multicultural Affairs, Undergraduate

Admissions, the School of Pharmacy and Health Professions, the Native American Studies Program, and the student-based Native American Association. All these entities have a history of outreach and community collaboration. This program is distinguished by its collaboration with many higher education institutions in Omaha and support from the Nebraska Tribes, the reservation schools, and a wide variety of Native American organizations. The Native American Retreat was designed with input and inclusion from Tribal Higher Education Programs, targeted reservation high schools, the Lincoln Indian Center, Indian Education Offices and local colleges such as the University of Nebraska at Omaha and Metro Community College. The program is held annually at Creighton University, so the participants are exposed to a university environment and interact with college students. In addition to designing a program that exposes students to college life, participants are exposed to Native American role models. Many of the participants have limited contact with Native American corporate and educational leaders. Furthermore, many of the events are interactive, so that the young Native American participants can see and learn by doing—a more traditional and comfortable method of learning for many Native Americans.

The Native American Retreat was founded on the belief that learning about choices and planning for a better future are powerful tools in fighting poverty. The program is designed to motivate Native American students to seriously consider higher education, prepare for a rigorous curriculum, and demonstrate that college is a viable option. In addition to designing a program that exposes students to college life, the program provides facilitated sessions on life issues, such as alcoholism or lack of spirituality, that could become barriers to their success. The program also explains college costs, scholarships, loans, and other ways of paying for college. As an encouragement to the students, some local businesses offer small scholarships to outstanding senior participants.

We identified reservation schools and Native American organizations to participate in our program. In turn, the schools and organizations selected students utilizing our selection criteria and application forms. We try to limit participation to sixty-five students and twenty adult chaperones.

We do not charge students or participating organizations to attend the Retreat, but the participating organizations are responsible for providing chaperones and travel expenses. Each organization is responsible for selecting serious participants utilizing the following criteria: the students must be Native American high school students who are responsible, cooperative, and who demonstrate good judgment, as verified by a teacher or counselor evaluation. Each student must be considering college, or a school representative must confirm that the student has college potential. The student must complete an application and essay. Thus the program identifies qualified and motivated students and requires that they go through a process similar to applying for college.

Participants and chaperones reside in our residence halls with the college students and experience college life for a three-day period. Participants have the opportunity to experience interactive career opportunity sessions, attend sessions on college preparation, and take part in planned cultural and social activities. Chaperones, the majority of whom are educators from the reservations and urban Indian areas, also receive training during the retreat.

The Native American Retreat is designed as an outreach program, but it also has the added benefit of serving as an excellent recruitment tool for Creighton. The students have an opportunity to come to campus and develop relationships with Creighton students, faculty, staff, and administrators. They can actually visualize themselves as Creighton students, and they become very familiar and comfortable on our campus.

Many of the participants have positive experiences that leave them with the desire to become a part of Creighton. Students who enroll at Creighton who were past retreat participants already have a well established relationship with Creighton students and personnel. They are very comfortable on campus and have a comfortable knowledge of Creighton and Creighton resources. The transition to Creighton is much easier. Since the inception of the retreat, we have had participants enroll every year at Creighton. In Fall 2003, 62% of the freshman Native American students were past retreat participants.

In addition to our formal retreat program, the college often establishes contact with students prior to enrolling. This is done through our outreach programs, then through scholarship workshops, or through cultural programming or other community outreach activities and speaking engagements. Creighton assists with the college application, financial aid and scholarship search, and applications. Once students have formally accepted a place at Creighton, we ensure that they are enrolled in programs and support services they are eligible for. We review their financial aid packages to make sure forms are completed and they receive the resources for which they are eligible. We then assist them with the registration process and informally attempt to cluster students together in classes.

Financial Support

In 1959, Creighton established full scholarships for Native American graduates of Red Cloud Indian High School on the Pine Ridge reservation in South Dakota. The Jesuits also run Red Cloud. In addition, Creighton annually provides one full-tuition, room-and-board Native American Diversity scholarship for an academically exceptional Native American student from Nebraska.

Over the years, Creighton has developed other support specifically for Native students. In 1999, former Creighton President Rev. Michael G. Morrison, S.J., through a group of generous benefactors, established the Morrison scholarship, which annually provides three renewable $5,000 scholarships for Native American students with a financial need. The Joseph & Marie Doll Vision Quest Endowment Fund offers a renewable $5,000 scholarship for Native American students based on need and academic achievement. The John T. Butkus Endowed Scholarship provides one-third tuition for a Native American dental student, and there are also several smaller Native-based scholarships available.

In addition to the University providing specific scholarships for Native American students, the Office of Multicultural Affairs, Admissions, Financial Aid, and Support Services work together to ensure students with high financial need have the resources necessary to enroll at the university. Once we have exhausted internal resources, we assist the students in finding and applying for external scholarships that will help them pay for the direct and indirect cost of college. Admissions and the Office of Multicultural Affairs conduct scholarship workshops to help the students apply for the larger and more complex scholarships. The Office of Multicultural Affairs constantly researches and locates additional scholarship resources that will help enhance our students' funding for school.

Student Retention

The success of our graduates and the support—financial, academic, and social—that we provide for our current students make us the school of choice for many Native American students in our region. In the 1999-2000 Creighton University Climate Survey, our Native American students reported high levels of satisfaction with the institution.

Once Native American students are enrolled, Creighton makes every effort to support and retain them by creating a welcoming environment and a community of Native scholars. The Office of Multicultural Affairs, Student Support Services, the Native American Association (NAA), the Jesuit community, Campus Ministry, and the Office of Minority Health Sciences all provide assistance to Native American students and help affirm the Native American culture within the Creighton environment. Creighton University is able to respond to Native American students on an individual basis, thereby personalizing the education process. In addition, we have a strong staff and faculty support network for Native American students. Creighton has reached out to women and minorities, admitting them in our educational and professional programs decades before legal mandates were in place. Creighton continues to collaborate, create, and sustain a campus environment that welcomes and nurtures talent from diverse perspectives.

Key to Creighton's success is the building of a supportive community of Native Scholars on the campus. Before Creighton's growing number of Native Americans, the rare Native student would feel quite isolated on the campus and generally that person would not complete the four years of study. This has changed over the years, as illustrated in the Table 1. Since 1995, Native

American enrollment has doubled. Freshman enrollment has consistently increased since 1994. Additionally, Creighton's Native American freshman enrollment consistently has a higher accepted applicant yield than any other ethnicity, with the highest yields ranging from 19% to 37% higher than the norm.

Table 1
Native American Enrollment, 1993-2002

Year	93	94	95	96	97	98	99	00	01	02
Arts and Sciences	15	15	14	14	16	14	19	22	26	28
Business	2	1	1	0	0	0	2	6	6	4
Nursing	1	0	0	0	3	2	2	6	3	3
Dentistry	1	1	2	3	4	3	1	1	0	1
Law	0	1	1	1	4	4	4	3	5	2
Medicine	2	2	2	3	2	3	3	2	6	7
Pharmacy and Health Professions	0	2	5	5	4	2	2	3	4	7
Graduate School	2	2	0	2	1	1	0	1	1	2
University College	2	1	4	3	5	4	4	3	3	3
Total	25	25	29	31	39	33	37	47	54	57

Source: Stephanie Wernig, Creighton University

Not only is increasing Native enrollment a sign of Creighton's progress, but retention and graduation rates also indicate that we are developing the elements for a strong program of retention. It is difficult to determine success with these numbers because they are so small; the true test will be over the next several years, as we find out if the larger classes are graduating. The real testimony is yet to be realized.

A key component for retention is the Office of Multicultural Affairs. The Office attempts to ensure that our students have every opportunity to develop their full academic potential by providing direct support and assistance to Native American students so that they may successfully complete their studies at Creighton. To achieve this goal, an important service we provide is academic advising and intervention. Academic advising is an ongoing process, and the coordinator of Multicultural Student Services provides relevant services through formal programs and ad hoc interactions. In addition to the direct support that the coordinator provides, she works with a network of resource providers in a system of support services. Early intervention consists of identifying at-risk students and providing assistance of various kinds, including enrollment assistance, scheduling assistance, classroom clustering, and financial and scholarship procurement.

This first phase of assistance is proactive in nature and is designed to increase retention by trouble-shooting problems and increasing the chance for a strong first semester by ensuring that students are in appropriate courses. Classroom clustering is a strategy implemented as a direct result of the feedback received from our focus groups conducted with Hispanic, African American, and Native American students. A theme emerged from these focus groups that under-represented minority students felt isolated and alienated in the classroom. They were often the only minority in their classes; therefore the coordinator implemented classroom clustering by placing incoming minority students together in specifically targeted classes. Students who were initially beneficiaries of this strategy reported a positive impact on their overall classroom experiences. The other benefit besides Native American students' confidence in expressing their opinions is the benefit majority students gain from the diverse opinions expressed in the classroom. Additionally, professors benefitted professionally by teaching to diverse students.

In addition to providing early preventative assistance, the coordinator has a formal process for intervening when students are not performing well. There are two systems at work. First the coordinator works with the Retention Director, who receives reports from faculty regarding performance and attendance issues. The next level of assistance is mid-term intervention. An aggressive system of contacting and meeting with students receiving a grade below a C in any class at mid-term is implemented. Upon meeting with a student, the coordinator works with the student to identify the problem(s) and provides support services and academic assistance based on the student's needs. This strategy allows one-on-one attention and assistance designed to help motivate as well as give the student the tools and direction needed to achieve success.

Another important part of retention is providing students with a concrete link between their course work and career exploration. The office works with students in the area of professional development through internships, employment in our office, and research opportunities. Often these links serve as a motivator and provide a strong connection between what they want to do in their career and their education.

To foster and encourage a strong connection among students and to the institution, we provide a variety of opportunities to form and build relationships. One basic method is a monthly potluck supper hosted by the Native American Studies Director. The Director builds community by hosting potlucks at his residence and having students come together to prepare the main course. The Director also invites faculty, Jesuits, and staff to come and interact with the students. In addition, local Native families are also welcomed to the gatherings, adding young and elderly people to the assembly and more closely replicating the social context of their own homes. Students also frequently bring non-Native friends to the gatherings. This has been a successful method of building relationships and allowing the students to feel connected to one another and the campus community.

The Native American Studies program, formally begun in 1999, is another important retention tool. The program itself is geared to collaborative service among Native peoples rather than simply an academic study of Native cultures, stressing collaboration with contemporary Native communities. There is no expectation that Native students enroll in the program or that the program is exclusively for Natives. What is important about the program in terms of retention is that Native students can see that the college has made room not only for them but also for the study of their cultures and history. This visibility is essential for our students. Several Native students have enrolled in the Native Studies program as a double major, and even if they never take a class the fact that the program exists has been consistently cited as an important factor for Native students coming to and staying at Creighton.

Training Leaders and the Native American Association

The Native American students at Creighton are committed to service and working with their Native American communities. The students are well-known leaders on and off campus, inspiring young Native Americans by serving as positive role models. The typical Native American Creighton student plans to work with Native communities after graduation. His or her plans are an obvious outgrowth of their commitment to Native communities and to each other while in college.

One important student organization on campus is the Native American Association (NAA), which helps build positive Native American leadership. The NAA leaders are usually a mix of new and seasoned leaders. The senior leadership encourages and promotes new leaders from the freshman and sophomore ranks. NAA is a social and cultural organization designed to bring students together for fun, friendship, cultural exchanges, and personal growth. NAA offers members opportunities to develop lifelong friendships, form a support system, plan major campus events, celebrate their various cultural traditions, develop their leadership skills, meet Native American leaders and role models, and get involved in making their college experience the best possible. In fact, the strong support network the students develop serves not only as a recruitment tool but also as a reason many students are retained.

One of NAA's goals is recruiting more Native Americans. NAA assists with ongoing recruitment through a variety of methods: writing letters, e-mailing, and telephoning prospective students. They even assist prospective students with their scholarship searches and maintain for our office a Native American Scholarship Directory. Other NAA recruitment activities include members going to their high schools to talk about Creighton and a direct marketing strategy of identifying and contacting prospective Creighton recruits. They are instrumental in the planning and implementation of the Native American Retreat. NAA leaders often plan and present entire sessions for the Retreat. They help recruit Creighton hosts and raise funds for the program. They are actively involved all three days and assist with Retreat evaluation.

Native Student Involvement at Creighton

Individually, Native American students at Creighton are represented in almost every arena. According to Nancy Kelsey, Creighton journalism major, "although their number remains small, Native American students at Creighton University are growing in visibility."[7] In addition to strong leadership in the Native American Association, our students are elected members of student government; involved in the school newspaper as writers, photographers, and photography editors; student athletes; and members of other cultural clubs and organizations and dance teams. Additionally, they are members of university-wide committees like the President's Council on Diversity, HARMONY Committee, and Committee on the Status of Women. They are also members of social fraternities and sororities and service organizations, past Service Trip participants and coordinators, and much more. "It's not like we're involved in just NAA," said Creighton journalism student, Tetona Dunlap, an Eastern Shoshone from Wyoming. "I am satisfied because [Native American students] hit upon a lot of different aspects of college everywhere from sports, to fraternities to school newspapers."[8]

What really demonstrates the quality of experiences and leadership exhibited by Native American students at Creighton is that a Native American student was recipient of the top honor bestowed upon a graduating senior, the Sprit of Creighton Award, for the last two years. The Spirit of Creighton Award is given annually to a male and female student who exemplify the mission and credo of Creighton University. Recipients are honored for their initiative, enterprise, academic achievement, and outstanding character traits. The fact that two Native American students have recently received this award demonstrates the positive experiences our Native students are having at Creighton and further illustrates how they are involved and valued.

Our students are creating positive contributions in transforming our campus, community, and world. A recent graduate received the 2003 Work Study Student of the Year Award. Two Native American Students were recipients of the prestigious Clare Boothe Luce Scholarship, and another received the top History award for a History major, the Allan M. Schleich Award. The students in the Native American Association also donated Native-related books to the Creighton library to amplify its general collection and to commemorate the start of the Native American Studies program by making a contribution to this scholarly effort.

Future Challenges

Although Creighton has made tremendous strides and has long-range goals for future improvement, the university is not where we would like it to be. Any strong recruitment and retention program for Native Americans faces the challenge of limited resources, financial and human, to sustain and enhance initiatives. As numbers increase and resources remain static, the challenge is sustaining the existing level of support. Existing initiatives must be institutionalized and a more formal process established for building leadership skills. The development of mentorship programs and the creation of opportunities for students to link with mentors in the professions they plan to pursue are long-range goals.

Creighton will need to expand its recruitment efforts throughout the United States. We need to develop relationships with targeted schools and create feeder schools in a variety of urban areas, reservations, and rural areas. At the same time, Creighton needs to educate its faculty about the realities of reservation and urban Native life so that they can better work with these students and appreciate their unique cultural and religious heritages. The Native American Studies Program is planning orientation trips for Creighton faculty so they can have first-hand experience of life on the reservation. There are over seven reservations within a day's drive of Creighton.

Ultimately, our best advertising is our integration into and acceptance by local Native communities and the success of our returning students. Because of a long difficult history between Natives and whites, our integration will take time, and trust must be built slowly and carefully. We must also recognize that the success of our students will not be judged by their communities by high salaries or prestigious titles but by their willingness to be of service to their people and to help their cultures thrive in the modern world while retaining the dignity and beauty of their traditions.

Notes

The authors of this article wish to thank Gertrude Lee (Navajo), who not only enriches the life of Creighton University but also assisted in the research for this paper. We also thank Dr. Stephanie Wernig in Student Services, who assisted with the statistics on student enrollment and retention.

1. Vincent V. Tinto, *Leaving College: Rethinking the Causes and Cures of Student Attrition* (Chicago: University of Chicago Press, 1987).
2. "Health Status of Racial and Ethnic Minorities in Nebraska," *Nebraska Department of Health and Human Services Preventive and Community Health*, April, 2002, 9.
3. Jodi Rave Lee, "There are no easy answers for teen suicides," *Lincoln Journal Star*, December 8, 2001, F4.
4. "Homicide and Suicide Among Native American 1979-1992," *Violence Surveillance Summary Series*, no. 2. National Center for Injury Prevention and Control. www.cdc.gov/ncipc/pub-res/natam.htm.
5. *Indian Country Today*, June 21-28, 1999.
6. "Characteristics of American Indians by Tribe and Language," in *1990 Census of Population* (Washington: U.S. Census Bureau, 1990), CP-3-7.
7. Nancy Kelsey, "Numbers Don't Count," *Reznet* (published by the University of Montana School of Journalism), October 5, 2002.
8. Kelsey, "Numbers Don't Count."

Notes on Contributors

JOAN E. BAILEY, Ph.D., is the senior vice president for Academic Affairs at the College of New Rochelle, a position she has held since 1997. She earned a Ph.D. in Philosophy and two master's degrees from Yale, and an undergraduate degree from Chatham College. Dr. Bailey joined the College of New Rochelle in 1974 as an instructor in the School of New Resources. In 1985, she was appointed assistant vice president and in 1990, associate vice president for Academic Affairs. In 1995, she became the dean of the School of Arts and Sciences. Her areas of specialization include interdisciplinary humanities, philosophy of education, ethics, and the problems of freedom.

RAYMOND A. BUCKO, S.J., Ph.D., is currently the director of the Native American Studies Program at Creighton University as well as an associate professor of Anthropology. He earned a Ph.D. in cultural anthropology from the University of Chicago, writing on contemporary Lakota (Sioux) culture and ritual practice. He taught for ten years at LeMoyne College in Syracuse. He is a consultant for the Ad Hoc Committee on Native American Ministry of the U.S. Catholic Bishops' Conference. He first worked with Native people in 1974 and has continued this ministry along with teaching and developing computer-facilitated teaching strategies. Father Bucko holds advanced degrees from Fordham University, the Jesuit School of Theology at Berkeley, and Regis College in Toronto.

ANTHONY J. CERNERA, Ph.D., has been the president of Sacred Heart University for fifteen years. He is a three-time graduate of

Fordham University, where he earned his doctorate in systematic theology. He continues to teach undergraduate and graduate students in related disciplines. He is a vice president of the International Federation of Catholic Universities, immediate past chairman of the Connecticut Conference of Independent Colleges, and a member of the board of directors of the Association of Catholic Colleges and Universities. Dr. Cernera is the editor of *Toward Greater Understanding*; *Vatican II: The Continuing Agenda; Continuity and Plurality in Catholic Theology*; and, with Oliver J. Morgan, two volumes *of Examining the Catholic Intellectual Tradition.*

LAWRENCE S. CUNNINGHAM, Ph.D., has been professor of Theology at the University of Notre Dame since 1988, and John A. O'Brien Professor of Theology since 2001. He earned his licentiate in Sacred Theology from the Gregorian University in 1961, and his Ph.D. in Humanities from Florida State University in 1969, where he was professor of Religion and Humanities for twenty-one years. Dr. Cunningham was presented the Paul Fenlon Teaching Award from the Men of Sorin College at the University of Notre Dame in 1989 and the Kaneb Teaching Award for Undergraduate Instruction in 1999. He was a founding member of the International Thomas Merton Society and chaired Notre Dame's Theology Department for five years. A prolific author and regular columnist in *Commonweal*, Dr. Cunningham has given more than 250 presentations for professional societies, colleges, and church groups.

CHARLES L. CURRIE, S.J., Ph.D., has studied at Fordham, Boston College, Woodstock College, and Cambridge University, gaining graduate degrees in philosophy and theology, and a doctorate in chemistry at the Catholic University of America. He taught at Georgetown, and was president of Wheeling College (now Wheeling Jesuit University) and of Xavier University, before returning to Georgetown to direct the University's Bicentennial Celebration in 1988 and 1989. Currently, he serves on the board (and executive committee) of the National Association of Independent Colleges and Universities, and chairs its secretariat.

Father Currie has been deeply involved in discussions concerning the application of the Vatican document on Catholic higher education, *Ex Corde Ecclesiae*, in the United States, and has traveled frequently to Rome for discussions with officials there. He has published and lectured widely on higher education. Most recently, he edited *Mission and Identity: A Handbook for Trustees.*

JOHN J. DEGIOIA, Ph.D., became Georgetown University's forty-eighth president in 2001. He began his professional career there after graduating from its College of Arts and Sciences in 1979, holding various leadership positions for more than two decades. Dr. DeGioia is a lecturer and faculty member in Georgetown's Department of Philosophy and has taught at Georgetown every year since receiving his doctorate from the Georgetown Graduate School of Arts and Sciences in 1995. As the University's first lay president, he works closely with the Georgetown Jesuit Community, home to nearly seventy priests and brothers. His wife, Theresa Miller DeGioia, is a Georgetown alumna and former staff member in the University's Office of Alumni and University Relations.

MARILOU ELDRED, Ph.D., became the tenth president of Saint Mary's College in 1997, the first lay woman to lead the institution. Since her inauguration, she has worked to maintain Saint Mary's position as one of the nation's premier Catholic women's colleges. Saint Mary's has earned a number one ranking from *U.S. News & World Report* five of her six years as president. She also helped to secure a $12 million grant from the Lilly Endowment for the development of a Center for Women's Inter-Cultural Leadership in 2001, the largest single gift in the College's history. Renewed cooperation between Saint Mary's College, the University of Notre Dame, and Holy Cross College, as well as a revitalized relationship with the South Bend/Mishawaka community, have also been hallmarks of her leadership.

ZENI FOX, Ph.D., received a master's degree in Religious Education and a doctorate in Theology from Fordham University. Her dissertation was titled "Lay Ministries: A Critical Three-Dimensional Study." An associate professor of Pastoral Theology at Immaculate Conception Seminary, Seton Hall University, she was also director of its Lay Ministry Program. Recent publications have included *New Ecclesial Ministry: Lay Professionals Serving the Church* and "The Vocation of Today's Lay Minister: Perspectives of a Teacher and Researcher" in *New Theology Review*. Dr. Fox plans workshops, conferences, and research to serve the needs of lay ministers.

SALLY M. FURAY, R.S.C.J., Ph.D., J.D., served as academic vice president and provost of the University of San Diego for twenty-five years, following administrative roles as dean of Arts and Sciences and chair of the English Department. She holds a doctorate in English and American literature from Stanford University, a J.D. degree from the University of San Diego School of Law, and has been a member of the California Bar for over thirty years. She was the first woman president of the Western College Association, board chair of the national Association of Catholic Colleges and Universities, vice president of the San Diego County Bar Association, and president of the board of governors of the San Diego Foundation. She is a member of the Legal Services Review Panel of the National Association of Independent Colleges and Universities. Among her honors are the Hesburgh Award from the Association of Catholic Colleges and Universities.

ALICE B. HAYES, Ph.D., has been the president of the University of San Diego since 1995, after six years as executive vice president, provost, and professor of Biology at Saint Louis University. She spent twenty-seven years at Loyola University of Chicago, where she held several senior positions. A biologist with a Ph.D. from Northwestern University, where she was a National Science Foundation Fellow, she has published numerous books and articles on the natural sciences and on Catholic higher education. As part of the People-to-People Citizen Ambassador Program, she participated in Botanical Delegations to South Africa, China, and the USSR. Dr. Hayes currently serves as a consultant/evaluator for the Western Association of the Commission on Institutions of Higher Education and is a member of the Executive Committee of the Association of Independent California Colleges and Universities.

DIANA L. HAYES, J.D., Ph.D., S.T.D., has been associate professor of Theology at Georgetown University since 1994. She served as an attorney for the Solicitor's Office (U.S. Department of Labor), the New York State Department of Social Services, and the New York State Consumer Protection Board. She earned a Doctor of Sacred Theology in 1988 from the Catholic University of Louvain and remains a theological consultant to the Office of Black Catholics, Archdiocese of Washington, the Secretariat for Black Catholics, USCCB, the Department of Education Sub-Committee on Catechesis and Cultures, USCCB, and the National Black Catholic Congress Office. Dr. Hayes is the recipient of numerous awards, including Georgetown University's Elizabeth Seton Medal for significant contributions to Catholic Theology, the 2001 U.S. Catholic Award for Furthering the Role of Women in the Church, and the Sr. Thea Bowman Award. Her recent books include *Were You There? Stations of the Cross*, and *Taking Down Our Harps: The Emergence of Black Catholics in the United States*. She is currently working on a handbook on liberation theologies.

MONIKA K. HELLWIG, Ph.D., has been executive director of the Association of Catholic Colleges and Universities since 1996. She earned a master's degree and her doctorate at Catholic University of America, and taught in the Theology Department at Georgetown University for nearly thirty years. Among her extensive writings are *Understanding Catholicism, Guests of God: Stewards of Divine Creation*, and *Whose Experience Counts in Theological Reflection?*

DENNIS H. HOLTSCHNEIDER, C.M., Ed.D., is executive vice president of Niagara University, and clinical associate professor of higher education at the State University of New York at Buffalo. He also teaches in the Institute for Administrators in Catholic Higher Education at Boston College. Father Holtschneider holds a doctorate in higher education administration from Harvard University. His recent publications include "Academic Ethics: State of the Field," in *Research in Ethical Issues in Organizations*, and "The Vincentian Tradition in U.S. Catholic Higher Education," in *As Leaven in the World: Catholic Perspectives on Faith, Vocation, and the Intellectual Life*.

KAREN M. KENNELLY, C.S.J., Ph.D., is a member of the Congregational Leadership Team of the Sisters of St. Joseph of Carondelet. She assumed this position in 2002, following experience as province director for the St. Paul Province of her congregation, and as president of Mount St. Mary's College, Los Angeles. She has served on the boards for the American Council on Education, the Association of Catholic Colleges and Universities, and the National Association of Independent Colleges and Universities, as well as serving as a trustee for a number of Catholic colleges, seminaries, and hospitals. Sister Karen's recent publications include "Faculties and What They Taught," in *Catholic Women's Colleges in America; Gender Identities in American Catholicism*, and "Women Religious in American Catholic History," for *The Encyclopedia of American Catholic History*. She holds a master's degree in history from CUA and a doctorate in history from the University of California at Berkeley. She served on the *Ex Corde Ecclesiae* Implementation Committee of the National Conference of Catholic Bishops from 1991-2000.

KEVIN E. MACKIN, O.F.M., Ph.D., is a priest of the Order of Friars Minor, Province of the Most Holy Name of Jesus. Since 1996, he has been the ninth president of Siena College. Father Mackin served as an assistant and associate professor of Religious Studies at Siena College, chairman of the department, and superior of its Franciscan community. The former president-rector of Christ the King Seminary, a graduate theological school in East Aurora, New York, he has held numerous leadership positions in his religious community. He earned four degrees from Catholic University of America: a bachelor's in Theology, a master's in Religious Education, and a licentiate and doctorate in Theology. He is an alumnus of the Harvard Institute for Higher Education. Father Mackin has served on various national, diocesan' and Franciscan committees on higher education and also on papal visitation teams of seminaries in the United States.

SHEILA MEGLEY, R.S.M., Ph.D., is a professor of English at Regis College and Salve Regina University. After earning a Master of Science degree in Financial Management/Accounting from Salve

Regina, she earned a Ph.D. from the University of Nebraska in English Literature. She is a CPA and has earned a master's degree in theology from Saint Xavier University. Sister Sheila was president of Regis College from 1992-2001 and held numerous leadership positions from 1974 to 1992 at Salve Regina. She also served at Saint Xavier University, Chicago, and Barat College, Lake Forest, Illinois. Among numerous national leadership positions, she is the vice chair-elect of the Association of Catholic Colleges and Universities.

MELANIE M. MOREY, Ed.D., has worked in the field of education and administration for the past twenty-eight years. She received her doctorate in higher education administration from Harvard in 1995. Dr. Morey works primarily as a researcher and consultant to Catholic colleges and religious congregations around issues of governance, sponsorship, leadership, and institutional identity. She is the founder and senior associate of Leadership and Legacy Associates. Dr. Morey is an adjunct professor of Higher Education at Villanova University and teaches in the Institute for Administrators in Catholic Higher Education at Boston College. She is the author of "The Way We Are: The Present Relationship of Religious Congregations of Women to the Colleges They Founded," in *Catholic Women's Colleges in America*. Together, Father Holtschneider and Dr. Morey have written "Keeping the Faith on Campus: Not the How, But Who," in *Commonweal*, and "Relationship Revisited: Catholic Institutions and Their Founding Congregations," in *Occasional Paper 47* (Washington: Association of Governing Boards).

WILLIAM J. SNECK, S.J., Ph.D., is associate professor in the Department of Pastoral Counseling, Loyola College, Baltimore. A member of the Society of Jesus since 1959, Father Sneck holds advanced degrees from St. Louis University, Woodstock College, and the University of Michigan. Certified as a Maryland State licensed psychologist, he has written and lectured on the relationship of psychology and religion and he is a member of the American Association of Pastoral Counselors, the American Psychological Association and Division 36, and the Society for the

Scientific Study of Religion. Father Sneck provides spiritual direction to faculty, staff, and students at Loyola as well as monthly peer-group supervision meetings for spiritual directors and pastoral counselors in the Baltimore area.

JOHN E. THIEL, Ph.D., is professor of Religious Studies at Fairfield University, where he has taught for twenty-seven years. He is also director of the University Honors Program and the author of five books, including *Senses of Tradition: Continuity and Development in Catholic Faith* and *Innocent Suffering: A Theological Reflection*. Twice a recipient of fellowships from the National Endowment for the Humanities (1989-90, 1997-98), Dr. Thiel is a member of the Catholic Theological Society of America and the American Academy of Religion, and serves on the Fundamental Theology Advisory Board of the international journal, *Concilium*.

Index